Other books by Jim Mullen:

My First Wedding

Baby's First Tattoo: A Memory Book for Modern Parents

It Takes A Village Idiot: Complicating the Simple Life

and

Paisley Goes with Nothing
 by Hal Rubenstein with Jim Mullen

What They Said About *It Takes a Village Idiot:*

"Fans of Steve Martin or Dave Barry will love it."
—Rocky Mountain News

"Funnier than *A Year in Provence*—like a hip *Green Acres*. Hilarious."
—Cleveland Plain Dealer

"With the humor he's known for in his 'Hot Sheet' column, Mullen explains how he was seduced by country life."
—New York Daily News

"Funny . . . As sophisticated as the classic *Mr. Blandings Builds His Dream House.*"
—Liz Smith, *Newsday*

"There's a master satirist at work in *Village Idiot.*"
—Virginian Pilot

NEWS INK INC.
www.newsinkinc.com

Copyright © 2011 by Jim Mullen

This is a work of fiction.
Most of the characters appearing in this work are fictitious.
Any resemblance to real persons, living or dead,
who are not related to me in some way, is purely coincidental.

Parts of this book first appeared in "The Village Idiot,"
a newspaper column syndicated by
Newspaper Enterprise Association, a division of United Media.

Designed by Terry Bradshaw

www.jimmullenbooks.com
ISBN 978-146-092-7793

Jim Mullen

NEWS INK INC.

Beach and Moan

"You're not wearing *that*, are you?" Sue was looking at me as if I were wearing a large flounder on my head.

"What?" I knew what she meant, but I wanted to hear her say it.

"That shirt."

That shirt? This shirt was one of my favorites. It was actually made in Hawaii. How often are you going to find a Hawaiian shirt made in Hawaii? Once in a lifetime? Twice? It is a work of art and my closet is a museum.

"It makes you look fat."

I looked in the mirror. The shirt did *not* make me look fat. My fat made me look fat.

Sue has said, "You're not wearing that, are you?" so often that I don't really hear it any more. Sometimes I think she would say it if I were wearing a tuxedo to a formal dinner at the White House.

"You're not wearing *that*?" she would say moments before we stepped out of the house, leaving me not enough time to change, but plenty of time to wonder if I was making some horrible fashion faux pas as we made our way through the D.C. traffic—like wearing white after Labor Day or leaving a price tag hanging off my sleeve.

The Hawaiian shirt had a bright unnatural blue background with large black and ivory colored leaf designs all over it. The word "bold" comes to mind. The words "devil-may-care" come to mind. The word "beachcomber" comes to mind.

"The words 'Hawaiian Punch cartoon character' come to mind," Sue said. "I think there's a ukulele in the attic, you want me to wait while you go get it?"

"Do you think it's too dressy? I could change into something more casual," I tossed back. I don't know if there really is anything more casual. No shirt at all, I suppose. Or maybe one of those hospital gowns that doesn't close in the back.

We were going to the neighbors for dinner. If you can't wear an aloha shirt to dinner with friends, where can you wear one? It's not as if I was wearing my pajamas to the office or a pair of buckskin trousers to a PETA rally.

"Didn't you get the memo?" I thought but did not say. "They've got this new thing now. It's called 'Casual Saturday.' Basically, it says I get to wear whatever I like and nobody can say anything about it, not even my wife. I'll e-mail you a copy. It's signed by Jimmy Buffet. You can see how casual clothes wrecked his career."

I know there are men out there who let their wives pick their clothes for them. I figure it's the first step towards having the complete sex change operation. Next comes the hormone therapy, then the breast implants, then the . . . well, never mind. Sorry, it's just not my thing. I didn't marry a woman so I could become one.

But it's not just that. Can you imagine a man saying to a woman, "You're not wearing that, are you?" Not twice, he wouldn't.

Sue knew I was not backing down on this. I had drawn a line in the laundry basket. I was wearing this Hawaiian shirt and that was the end of the discussion.

"Wait a minute," she said and went back upstairs. In two minutes she was back, wearing a Hawaiian shirt of her own. Bolder and sillier.

"Oh no," I said, "I don't want to be one of those couples that dresses like twins. People will make fun of us behind our backs."

"Don't worry about it," she said, "I'm sure they already do."

Fear of Phoning

The first of this month's many phone bills just arrived. It was for $192.18. It used to be that I only got one phone bill a month. From a place called the phone company. Now I get five bills a month—one for the landline, one for the cell phone, one from the long distance provider on the landline, one for my internet service provider and one for the DSL service—from companies with made-up, ultramodern names like Vermaxtel, Instacomm, Qualtext and Spurt. They're all run by the same guys who used to run the phone company. And they're always merging. Next month Instacomm and Qualtext will merge and become "Commquat, a voice-data resource service." Or, as we say in English, a phone company. You and I won't be able to tell the difference, but two former Instacomm and Qualtext executives will be buying themselves $12 million ski chateaus in Banff.

My cell phone bill is supposed to be $85 a month. As I recall, my cell phone provider and I had a big ceremony in the middle of the shopping mall when we signed the contract binding me to this deal for two years. We swore solemn oaths to each other; we signed reams of official looking documents; we took a blood test. It was touching; all it lacked was candles and flowers and a cell phone agreement photographer. We had everything but a minister and close relatives. We hugged, and I took my new cell phone away with a tear in my eye.

I have yet to get a bill for $85. The smallest one was for $141.44. Mind you, I didn't use the cell phone at all that month. It gets no reception in my house. I only use it for emergencies. In addition to the $85 monthly fee was tax on the phone, a gross receipt surcharge, a 911 fee, Federal Tax, state sales tax and county sales tax, and of course, the Federal Universal Service and Regulatory Fee which is not to be confused with the aforementioned Federal Tax. Was any of this mentioned at in our cell phone pre-nup? Certainly not. I felt like a new bride who doesn't find out until after she says, "I do" that the three small children from his previous marriage will be living with them.

What I enjoy most is that Commquat doesn't want you to call them if there is a question about the bill. They want you to use their Internet site. It's worrisome when the last thing your phone company wants you to do is phone them. It cannot be a good omen.

Sure enough, I tried calling and couldn't get through. My call, a tape said over and over, was very important to them. Just not important enough to answer. I wanted to ask about some things on my bill. Like what was the fourteen-cent charge for printing the bill all about? Is the fifty-two-cent chargè for complaining about the bill on there every month, or just the months when I complain? Are they kidding about the three-dollar-and-twelve-cent charge to pay for the merger of Instacomm and Qualtext or what?

I finally went to their website. I had to fill out all kinds of personal information and get a password. Why? Do they think that someone pretending to be me is going to go on-line and pay my bill for me? Maybe they want to make sure that it's me complaining, not an impostor. Finally I logged in and up popped a message.

"Would you like more information on how the proposed merger between Commquat and Spurt will affect your cell phone service?" No. I went to the next screen.

"Would you like more information on how the class action suit filed by Qualtext stockholders will affect your service?" No, on to the next.

"Would you take a few minutes to fill out a customer satisfaction survey? If not, we will fill out the form for you." On to the next.

"If you did not find the answer to your question here, please call us during our business hours, 9:30 to 9:45 A.M., Mondays, Thursdays, and the first Wednesday of the month." I can't call them then; those are the same hours my cell phone divorce lawyer keeps.

Living Will Is
the Best Revenge

The nurse asked me if I had a Living Will. "Yes, I do," I said.

"Did you bring it with you?"

"No, I didn't."

"Why not?"

"Well, I'm only here to have my teeth cleaned. I didn't really think I'd need it."

I could see if I was having a filling, or a wisdom tooth pulled, but a cleaning? Was it really that life-threatening?

There was much consternation behind the counter. Could they possibly proceed at all without the Living Will? Do I really look that old? Is it like that annoying teenager who always gives me the Senior Discount down at the Shop and Spend on Tuesdays? I want to tell her she's just given me a fifteen-percent discount for being prematurely gray but I just take it and shut up.

I can't even remember what the provisions of my Living Will are. Did I tell Sue to pull the plug the day I couldn't remember what was in my Living Will, or did I tell her to keep me alive until I was smaller than any of the tubes coming out of me? I can't even remember where it is. Where do you put something like that? On the refrigerator door? In my home office? I can't find the phone bill in my home office. Or the phone. I don't need a Living Will, I need a Living Filing Clerk.

I do remember meeting with my lawyer and drawing up the papers. He said, "You should have a Living Will so that if you're incapacitated your wishes will be carried out."

"My main wish is that I shouldn't be incapacitated."

"You should have thought about that before you decided to eat right and exercise. If you had listened to me, you would have been dead by now and not have to worry about all this. Half my business is estate planning. The other half is divorces."

"You mean people still have estates after they divorce? That's a comfort. It must be nice, getting all that money for filling out a few forms of lawyer mumbo-jumbo."

"I plan the estates for the half that didn't get divorced. And it's not just a little form; there's a lot involved," said Mumbo Jumbo, Esq. "For example, do you have a Health Care Proxy?"

"Of course not. I'm married. Besides, at my age . . ."

"Proxy. Not *Doxy*, you pathetic old goat. Turn up the hearing aid, would you? Do you have a will?"

"I don't think I need one. Everything's held jointly."

"Yeah, but what if you both die in a plane crash? Where's your money go then?"

"You're just trying to cheer me up, aren't you?"

"Say you both die in a flaming car crash? Who gets your estate then? I get this stuff all the time. If some of my clients only knew what happened to their estates after they died, they would be turning over in their graves."

"Have you ever thought of becoming a motivational speaker?"

"So let's talk about your Living Will. For example, you're completely conscious, but you can't move. Would you want them to take extraordinary measures to keep you alive?"

"No, I'd want them to take extraordinary measures to make me move."

"Sorry, that's not on the form. Let's say someone has to cook all your food, constantly clean up behind you, run all the errands and do all the chores while you sit in bed all day and watch television because you can't do the simplest things for yourself. Would you want them to use extraordinary means to keep you alive?"

"That's pretty much the way I live right now. I'd want them to take extraordinary means to keep whoever's doing all that for me alive."

"That would be your wife. She, however, wants to pull the plug."

"When I'm incapacitated?"

"No. Right now."

I've Got Mail!

Dear Mrs. Abacha,

Wow! It's not everyday I get an e-mail all the way from Nigeria. I can't tell you what a surprise that was. Let me say that normally I'd jump on your offer to take 30% of the $25 million your late husband left in a Swiss bank, but unfortunately, an Oliver Kabila, of the Congo, has offered me 30% of $168 million which his late father left in a bank in Geneva. His father, like your husband, also died under suspicious circumstances, and like you, he can't trust anyone in his country to handle the $168 million. For wealthy people, I have to say, you guys sure don't seem to have many friends.

Oliver's story is amazingly similar to your story, wouldn't you say? And that you both need my help on the same day! What a coincidence. It's feast or famine, isn't it? Here I am wondering where I am going to get the money to buy a new set of snow tires and you guys come along. This morning a Dr. Kayode Adeyemi of the Union Bank of Liberia offered me thirty percent of $17 million and a Dr. Isa Mustapha of Togo wanted me to help him with $22 million that was left in his bank by a man who has no heirs to claim it. I'm not even going to answer their e-mails for that kind of chump change.

The way they write English, it sounds as though you may all have been taught by the same guy. Not that your English isn't excellent; you speak English much better than I can speak, well, whatever it is you speak over there. If you do know each other, please call Dr. Adeyemi and Dr. Mustapha and tell them my answer is a firm "no."

Let me say right here how sorry I was to hear about your husband General Abacha's untimely death. He sounds like he was a swell guy. It couldn't have been easy to amass a $25 million fortune in a poverty-stricken place like Nigeria, but it shows what you can do with a little elbow grease and moxie.

I have to say, politics seems to pay much better in Nigeria and the Congo than it does over here. The President of the Congo has $168 million in the bank? That's amazing because we're a much bigger country than the Congo and I don't think any of our politicians make that kind of money. That's why we must keep this deal secret. If our politicians ever find out what your politicians are getting paid in Nigeria and the Congo, they're sure to ask for a raise.

I still don't understand how you got my name but when it comes to high finance, you got the right guy. I know almost all the tellers at our bank. There's Erna, Betty, Tanya and Fred. Fred could give them all beauty tips but that's another story. Boy, won't they be surprised when I walk in with $168 million. I'll have to tell them I sold something on eBay so they won't get suspicious.

I have already told Oliver that 30% of $168 million can in no way cover my costs and I am suggesting a 60/40 split (me getting 60, of course). I just wanted you to know, Mrs. Abacha, that as much as I would like to help you, I don't think it would be fair to Mr. Kabila to take on another client at this time.

Just because I can't help you doesn't mean you should give up hope. You should keep trying. With any luck you may be able to find one or two more e-mail addresses of people who might be able to help you. I'd be very careful about sending your letter out to people you don't know, though. You never know what kind of nuts are out there. Some of them may even try to scam you out of your money. Be careful.

Your friend,

Jim

Let's Put The "Fun" Back In "Funeral"

We just got back from a huge family reunion. Or as some people like to call it, a funeral. We haven't had this much fun in ages. We saw people we hadn't seen in years: aunts, uncles, first cousins, second cousins, cousins forcibly removed. Bob's first wife's brother and Bill's high school buddy Jack, the doctor who delivered Sue, and in-laws from the out-of-town side of the family.

People say funerals make you think about your own mortality, but what they really make you think about is other people's mortality.

"I thought Ed looked good. For being on chemo. You can hardly tell that's a wig."

"I didn't know Shirley was still alive. How old is she now? A hundred and eight?"

We drank like underage college kids on Spring Break in Cancun. Hey, we're in mourning; what's *their* excuse? It was so much fun that many of us are hoping someone else dies soon so we can do it again. But next time we'll do a few things differently.

Next time we'll get a hotel room. We tried but you know how relatives are—they get all huffy and offended if you don't stay with them. It's worse than fighting over the check at a restaurant.

"Stay in a hotel? What's wrong with you? You'll stay with us, we won't hear of anything else." Big mistake.

You don't have to leave the bathroom the way you found it in a hotel. You can let the water run. You don't get scalded when you're in the shower and someone on the other side of the house flushes a toilet. You don't have to make the bed in a hotel. You can stay up till all hours and watch any channel on TV you want, and not just the Weather Channel.

Nieces and nephews won't wake you up at 6 A.M. in a hotel. Coughing, hacking, runny-nosed, grabby, touchy little nieces and nephews. They've just given me every disease that's going around second grade this week. It's no longer the common cold. It's mutated into something that's a cross between ebola and the plague. "That's what probably carried their Grandpa off in the first place," I think (but don't say).

You can order room service in a hotel. Somehow I can't see my sister-in-law wheeling a cart down to our room every morning filled with Eggs Benedict and double lattes. Besides, she's busy making food for the wake.

Let's see, we've had a memorial, a church service, a viewing, a sitting, a luncheon, and a dinner. She's now making something to take to the wake. All the relatives that haven't yet moved to Florida are making something that two hundred-plus people can nibble on: ribs, hams, sausages, pastries, pies, and cakes. Not a vegetable in sight.

"It's comfort food," says Sue. Yes, a comfort to the pharmaceutical industry. Three days of that and I'm about to die myself. Invest in whoever makes defibrillators.

No matter what they say, rent a car. "What do you need to rent a car for? You're only going to be in town a few days. We'll pick you up at the airport. We'll take you anywhere you want to go." Big mistake. I'd like to go antiquing. I'd like to go golfing. I'd like to go see the Will Ferrell movie where he prances around in his underwear. Any of them. But you can hardly ask the bereaved to run you over to the multi-plex while they're in mourning. Yet if we had stayed in a hotel and rented a car, who would be the wiser? Instead we sit at some relatives' hushed home, stare at each other and say things like, "It's sad that the only time we get together like this is when someone dies," when we really want to say "It'd be sadder if they didn't get together. If no friends and family got together at your funeral; if no one laughed about the silly things you did when you were alive, if they didn't remember your practical jokes, if they didn't relish rehashing your most embarrassing moments, that would be sad. Hell, I'd rather go to a funeral."

Happy Holidays
from the Fergusons

Dear Friends and Family,

Happy Holidays! If you're saying to yourself, "That doesn't look like a picture of the Fergusons on the front of the card," you're right. There was a bit of a mix-up down at the photo store but it was too late to have the cards done over. As you know, Bob and I only have two kids, not four, and neither of us have ever been skiing but other than that, it's not a bad picture. And we got them for half-price, which is a good deal because we've had to watch our pennies ever since Bob got downsized. But we still wonder: who's sending out *our* pictures this holiday?

Sorry we haven't written sooner but neither of us has been in much shape to write this year. I donated a kidney to my brother-in-law Joe but he rejected it. It turns out he needed a liver. I always get those two mixed up. Liver, kidney, kidney, liver, what's the big difference? We had a good laugh about it and I'm happy to say that Joe died with a smile on his face. Sometimes laughter *is* the best medicine.

Josh and Amber both got into the community college. Josh is majoring in Body Piercing and Amber is waffling between Assistant Nail Technician or Tattoo Artist. As you know, there were times when I thought they'd never get out of high school. I kept telling them and telling them, "If you don't get good grades you're not going to amount to anything." They're glad I nagged them now.

Bob's dad only has to wear the ankle restraint for another three months and then he's off house arrest. He still swears he has no idea what happened to the church's money and that he's just the fall guy. He's already planning a nice long vacation in the Cayman Islands as soon as he gets out.

Bob's working at the Big Pig BBQ until another "employment opportunity" comes along. The manager is pretty happy with his work because he says a lot of times older people aren't quick enough to work in the fast-food business. Funny, I never thought forty-six was all that old. Yet even at his advanced age, he thinks they may make him afternoon grill manager.

It seems my job as a grief counselor isn't recession-proof either. After their first consultation with me, more and more people find they have the courage to face this most difficult time alone. When they leave my office almost all of them thank me and say, "You've made me realize that it could be worse. Much, much worse." I guess you can say I'm doing God's work.

Bob's mother is living with us now and it's like having an extra pair of helping hands every day. She's too frail to actually do anything, but she does what she can to motivate people. "Who taught you how to do dishes?" she might say, or "You call that a pie crust?" The kids just love her. If she forgets to say, "Are you going out looking like that?" when they leave the house they feel neglected. Everyone loves her, she's such a people person.

We don't hang stockings over the Yule Log anymore since the accident last year. Who knew a sock could burn like that? Not Fluffy, that's for sure. Most of her fur has grown back but she still won't sleep on the mantel like she used to. That's about it for us, but here's wishing you'll have as happy a holiday as we will this year.

—The Fergusons

Bride or Groom's Side of the Story

Sue and I have stopped going to wedding receptions. We got tired of sitting in front of the speakers. The bride and groom seem to think we've made some special request to be deafened by the band. It's always so loud we can't speak to each other, much less the other guests. We sit and smile and nod while the bride's father is talking to us. "Ain't that the truth," "I know what you mean," and "You can say that again," we say over and over because we cannot hear a word he's saying. The only thing we have to go on is the expression on his face. For all we know, he is complaining about the loud music, too. The music is not just loud, it's bad. It has been picked especially to annoy me.

I wouldn't like this crap at a normal volume. Now that it's making my hair blow in the breeze from the speakers I *really* hate it. I don't know what message the happy couple thinks they are sending us, but the message I'm receiving is "Give us an expensive present and get the hell out. My parents made me invite you. They said you might be good for a cappuccino machine."

Which brings up another sore point. We may stop giving presents, too. When we were still going to weddings there was always the slim chance that the happy couple might still be married by the next time we saw them, say a few weeks later at the baby shower. No more. More than once we have gotten an invitation to the second wedding before we have gotten a "Thank You" note for the first. We will run into the bride's parents at the grocery store and find out that the first husband's gone, she's got two kids under two and they are in an expensive custody battle over his frozen sperm. He never spent any time with the kids when they were married, which is why they're getting divorced (that, and his new girlfriend). Now he's suing for full and complete custody; he can't bear to be away from the little dears for a single moment.

"And by the way, she really likes the cappuccino machine you gave them. She's just a little late with the 'thank you' notes. She's been so busy going to all her girlfriends' second weddings, don't you know. She can't wait to see you at her next wedding, though. This time she's registered at Jacoby and Meyers. And she wants you to know they've hired a really good local band, Thunder and Lightning. It's the only group in the tri-state region with two drummers."

It also annoys us that getting a wedding invitation is like getting a bill for something you didn't buy and don't want.

"We got an invitation to Jyoti and Chad's wedding. It says, 'Please save the date—December 24th.'"

"Gee, what could that conflict with?"

"It will be on Anguilla with the reception to follow."

"Why don't they just send us a card that says, 'We don't want you at our wedding, but we would like you to send an expensive gift. Getting married in Anguilla isn't cheap.'"

Not that we would have gone if Jyoti and Chad's wedding was being held next door. It's nothing personal, it's just that Sue and I have decided never to go to another wedding as long as we both shall live. Maybe the banns of marriage should ban marriage.

Newspapers are partly to blame. Every week they print wedding announcements that tell what the bride wore, where it took place, the name of the officiant, what the bridegroom does, who their parents are and what they do. It all sounds so wonderful—who wouldn't want to get married? But what if the newspaper made all newlyweds agree to publish a "Marriage Update" every five years or so? Something like this would surely be more effective:

MILFORD — TROUT

Jenny Milford, daughter of Sally and John Milford of Middletown, and Everly Trout, son of Elma and Vernon Trout of Littleville were married in June 2006.

"Why she wanted a big church wedding I'll never know," said her soon-to-be-ex-mother-in-law. "As far as we know that was the first and last time she's been in a church. I told Everly he was too young, but who ever listens to me?"

Jenny Trout says she was never so happy in her life—for about the first year and a half.

"Then, while I'm pregnant with the second baby Everly started staying out every night drinking with his old high school buddies. If he wants to be single, fine. Go be single. Go marry one of your floozies and make her life miserable."

The Trouts have two children, Verna and Mava, and are still paying for their honeymoon cruise to the Bahamas.

The Hiltons' Guide to Raising Children

Raising happy, well-adjusted children isn't easy. You'll have some sleepless nights, but in the end, remember, if you do it right, you'll be the first people they call for bail.

Hire the Right Nanny

A lot of people think a nanny should be trained in child psychology, nursing, and nutrition. But we found that a pretty blond with big boobs works just as well, even if she can't speak English. It keeps dad happy and when he's happy, everybody's happy.

Tough Love

Children are always testing you. Give them an inch and they'll take a mile. That's why it's so important to put your foot down. But you have to be creative, you have to make the punishment fit the crime. Once, we told Paris that we'd fire her maid if she wouldn't let her in to clean her room. And we did, too. Paris cried for almost five minutes but she learned a big lesson. Which is: don't become too attached to the help.

Self-Esteem

Give your child a unique name, something that is hers alone. Like naming her after the city where she was conceived. There's nothing quite like the look on an eleven-year-old's face when she figures out how she got her name. There's nothing like the emotions that will run through you the first time you hear your child say, "Ewww, that's so gross! What if my friends find out?" Priceless.

Set Limits

We suggest three or four million dollars a year. If you give children more than that, they'll think money grows on trees when we all know it really comes from grand-daddy.

Respect Your Children's Privacy

Don't go snooping around Face Book trying to find sex videos starring your children. Those videos are extremely private and meant only for their three or four million closest friends. Looking at them means you are no better than the stalkers, strangers, the Russian mafia and lonely men on oil-drilling platforms who have already seen them.

Emphasize the Value of an Education

Explain to your children that if they don't learn math, they might accidentally over tip. If they don't study geography, they'll never know the difference between a vacation in Capri and one in Majorca. If they don't study history, they won't know how Columbus discovered Plymouth Rock.

Communication

Communication between parents and children is crucial. Many problems are caused by simple misunderstandings. Whenever we're going to be globe-hopping for more than a couple of months, we almost always leave the kids a note on the fridge door. "See you next March," or something like that so they'll know how much we care.

Set Boundaries

Your rules may be different, but we always make sure that the Middle East and North Korea are "off limits" for our children unless they're with someone we know or with someone who's really famous.

Know Their Friends

Are your children hanging around with the wrong crowd, picking up bad habits? All too often we run into parents who don't realize that a child's friends have more influence on them than their parents do. All our children's friends have been to the best drug and alcohol rehab centers in the country. They are top notch. It just makes common sense—they're our children, we owe them the very best.

34

Pick Your Battles

Does every conversation with your child turn into a fight? Why not do what we do? Go shopping. In Milan. Or Tokyo. There's nothing like a spending spree to cheer everyone up. Or go to a spa together for a week or two. Take a break from all life's little ups and downs.

Discipline

Sometimes, you have to lay down the law. Which is why we have a lawyer on retainer just for that reason. We call him whenever the children misbehave and he gives them a good talking-to. Then we send them to the house in Cabo to let them think about what they've done.

Is Food Good for You?

On the nightly news last night—in the middle of the constipation, heartburn, erectile dysfunction, high blood pressure, diabetes, and arthritis remedy ads—there was a story that claimed eating vegetables might be the cure for constipation, heartburn, erectile dysfunction, high blood pressure, and diabetes. Some government agency released a report that said eating vegetables may increase my heart function, improve my digestion, lower my risk of getting cancer, and let me stay healthier longer.

How do they allow such quackery on television without even a disclaimer at the end explaining the pitfalls of eating vegetables? Where's the "May cause flatulence, loss of body fat, regular bowel movements, increase in energy and sweet, baby-sweet breath" warning at the end? They didn't even say that I should contact my doctor before starting to eat a diet that includes vegetables or that pregnant women should consult their physicians before eating vegetables. Is that legal? Have vegetables gotten FDA approval? Has there been any lab testing on them? I've been to my pharmacy a thousand times for heart medicine and blood pressure medicine and I've never once seen any vegetables on the shelf. But get this—you can buy them over the counter at practically any grocery store! You don't even need a prescription.

It's all part of Big Farma's diabolical plan to wean us off drugs and pills and make us eat roughage and unprocessed food. They use a thousand smarmy marketing tricks to get our kids hooked on vegetables. They grow vegetables in a lot of different flavors, like children's vitamins, just to make them taste good. What a cheap and sleazy ploy that is. Thankfully, most people don't fall for it.

And what are the dangerous side effects of eating vegetables? We'll never know. Why? Because there are there no nutrition labels on vegetables! How many calories do they contain? How much trans-fat? How much sodium? They don't tell us; there's no nutrition label on a tomato.

What are they trying to hide? When I take a fistful of pills, I don't have to worry about counting calories. Are vegetables deadly? Some reports say that if you eat fifty pounds of carrots a day it will kill you, yet they let school kids eat them.

Most important, where do vegetables come from? Are they made in big, clean sanitary factories like my heartburn medicine? Are they made in giant, government-inspected facilities like my constipation medicine? No, they are not. Most people would be surprised to learn the unbelievable truth—that almost all vegetables come from filthy, dirt-covered fields! Dirty, dirty, dirty places called farms. Some of them, like potatoes, are even *buried* in the dirt. You don't even want to know what some of Big Farma's farmers spread on their fields to help them "grow" their vegetables.

Many vegetables are crawling with insects. If you can believe this, it's how many of them are "fertilized." It's disgusting and yet it doesn't prevent Big Farma from making dubious health claims about them.

What are their interactions with real medicines? What are the risks involved? Is it OK to eat vegetables if you have high blood pressure? Diabetes? Heartburn? Are vegetables covered by your medical insurance? No. You have to bear the entire cost of your vegetables. One hundred percent. If they were beneficial, wouldn't your insurance company pay for them? And how do vegetables get to market without going through the same rigorous, double-blind testing that got us Zetia, Vioxx and fen-phen? Would you let your family eat a bunch of untested, untried vegetables? Do you want to be the guinea pig for that?

Farmers with their quack claims about the health benefits of vegetables are taking high-paying jobs away from the American pharmaceutical industry and from medical professionals. Write your congressperson and ask them why vegetables don't have to undergo the same rigorous testing as Prilosec and Metamucil.

It wasn't long ago that hundreds of people were sickened by eating vegetables in a chain restaurant. A lot of them ate dishes with tomatoes in them, but some of them said they didn't. So, it's got to be the tomatoes, right? It couldn't possibly be the minimum-wage busboy who didn't wash his hands after using the restroom because he already washed his hands once today. It must be the tomatoes.

It couldn't be the grabby three year-old behind you who crawled on the floor, then sucked his fingers, then touched everything he could reach on his way out; if he got sick, it's got to be the tomatoes.

It can't be the ice they put in your soda just because it comes from an ice machine that hasn't been cleaned since the day it was first installed; it's got to be the tomatoes.

It couldn't have been the guy who sneezed as he walked past your table without covering his nose; it must be the tomatoes.

It couldn't come from touching the menus that have been handled by every customer that's ever been in the place as well as the staff. There's no way that could transmit germs; it's got to be the tomatoes.

It's not the cash you just got out of the ATM machine, or the change in your pocket. Everyone knows there's a secret ingredient in money that kills germs on contact and that no matter how many people with filthy hands touch it, it can't transmit disease; it's got to be the tomatoes.

It can't come from the French fry your boyfriend snatched from the pile on your plate with the same hands he had been using to clean the fish tank twenty minutes ago; it's got to be the tomatoes.

It's not the hamburger you ate with your bare hands after driving the rental car you picked up at the airport two hours ago. Because we all know they always disinfect those steering wheels; it's got to be the tomatoes.

It couldn't be touching the snot-encrusted Game Boy that Junior and his little brother were fighting over all morning that you finally snatched and put in your purse so they wouldn't fight at the table; it's got to be the tomatoes.

It wasn't the diaper you just changed in the rest area family room; it's a well-known fact you could eat off the floor in those places. It's got to be the tomatoes they put on your BLT.

It couldn't be the plastic utensils in those little buckets in the company cafeteria. Sure, it's hard to grab one fork without touching two of the others, but one little touch can't spread germs. It's not like they're tomatoes.

It couldn't come from the telephone. Sure, every time you touch it you're practically sucking up someone else's dried spit, but we all know it's the tomatoes. What else could it possibly be?

There's no way disease could be spread by children. Talk to any parent or teacher and they'll tell you they rarely get sick during the school year. It's only when they eat, touch, or walk past a tomato that they start to feel ill.

Whoops! Wait a minute. The FDA just announced it's perfectly safe to eat tomatoes. It turns out that they're actually *good* for you! Go figure. Thank goodness this scare didn't put every tomato grower in the country out of business—it just cost them tens of millions of dollars that they'll never get back.

What I Did on My Summer Staycation

This year Dad said we couldn't afford to go anywhere farther than the backyard because of the gas prices. It took Dad two days to get the RV into the backyard, but when he did it was great.

Camping in the RV is a lot of fun. Dad lets us watch videos there that Mom would never let us watch at home. One day I watched all three *Shrek*s in a row. And he lets us wear the same clothes two and three days in a row. Mom wanted to go on vacation with us, but she said she had to stay home and work. Sometimes she'd come out to see us, but most of the time after work she would stay in the house. She said that was vacation enough for her.

Last year we went to the Grand Canyon. It was really great. The best part was that they have donkeys you ride down to the bottom. Donkeys are like horses but they have stupider names, like Sally and Buttercup. No cowboy would ever ride a horse named Buttercup so I said I wouldn't ride down there until they gave me a boy donkey. The guide came over and looked at my donkey and said, "What stupid cowboy told you that was Buttercup? That's not Buttercup, that's Jolly Roger. Buttercup doesn't have a white spot on her forehead." I felt sorry for the stupid cowboy because everyone laughed at his mistake.

Sometimes Rudy, who lives across the street from us, would come over to hang out. He was on vacation, too. His Dad filled up their back yard with sand and put up a volleyball net. We would go over there sometimes and Mr. Delfino says it's the best vacation he's ever had. He says he may never mow the lawn again. Once, Mrs. Delfino yelled at him for tracking sand through the house but he didn't seem to care. He said she should come out and let him rub some sunscreen on her back. It didn't sound funny to me, but she laughed.

My sister Halley just turned fourteen and she is so snooty. She acts like she's fifteen. She and Dad fight all the time. "I need a real vacation," she said. Dad said, "A vacation from what? The mall? I tell you what, how'd you like a vacation from that cell phone for a few weeks? I can make that happen." She made a face and went into her room and locked the door. It made me remember how much she hated the Grand Canyon because her cell phone didn't work there.

On the way to the Grand Canyon we stopped to see my grandma and that was fun, because she lived in the Olden Days before they had video games and chicken wings. She says kids didn't used to talk back then and they knew what the word "no" meant. That must have been a long, long time ago. I asked her what her favorite hip hop music was and she said they didn't have music like that when she grew up. She said the TV only had three channels and they didn't have DVDs. They didn't have anything when she was a kid. She must have been really poor. I told her she could use my iPod if she wanted to, but she said she wouldn't know how to use it. What's to know? You turn it on and scroll through your playlists.

"What did you guys do for fun?" I asked her. She said they made cookies and pies in a bowl; you didn't buy them in a store. I thought she was joking but she said she'd thought she'd make some cookies right now. It was fun. Kinda. Especially the part where you lick the spoon. If you don't lick the spoon, the cookies won't come out right or something. Even Halley liked the cookies and she doesn't eat practically anything.

We couldn't visit Grandma this summer, so I called her and told her that if she wanted to have some fun too, just make some cookies and send them to me. And she did. They were OK, but they weren't the same. I think she forgot to have someone lick the spoon.

Post More Bills

After a public outcry, the honchos at Major League Baseball decided not to let a movie company put ads on the first, second and third base bags. Some things are sacred. Why, if they allowed that kind of advertising in places like Coors Field, Qualcomm Stadium, Minute Maid Park, or Network Associates Coliseum, it might cheapen the entire sport. Besides, ads on the bases might distract fans from the twenty-foot-tall beer, shaving cream, and cell phone ads along the outfield fence. And it would be an affront to all the people in the stands wearing t-shirts and hats splashed with company logos and brand names and pictures of rock stars. They might miss the ad on the ticket stub that can be used as a coupon to get a dollar off a large, frozen pizza at the local big box store. Fans might miss the ad on the paper hot dog tray for the place that will change your oil and give you a free lube job with every $19.95 super wash. Advertising on the bases? An outrage! Please! Stop! Laughing! By the way, this post-game paragraph was brought to you by a subdivision of a giant multinational brewer who pretends to be a fledgling Mexican micro-brewery even though that beer comes out of the same vat as all the rest of it.

We see so many ads that, like common viruses, we develop an immunity to them. So advertisers are always looking for new spots, new ways to get their message across. Eighteen-wheel trucks that used to be painted white or silver are now huge rolling billboards. It keeps painters employed and the trucks neat so what's the harm? In big cities, the subways are covered in advertising; the revenue is used to lessen the taxpayer's burden. I'm bringing this up because it strikes me that one place where advertising might break new ground and also benefit consumers is in the funeral trade. Why can't the dearly departed's favorite beer or his favorite team help sponsor his final rest? Let's say a baseball fan dies. He may not want *Spiderman IV* advertised on the bases, but surely he wouldn't mind having Chief Noc-A-Homa plastered all over the side of his coffin. Especially if it substantially lowered the price. Remember those telephones in the shape of footballs? Why not get buried in one? With plastics, they can make coffins in any shape at all. Imagine a giant six-foot-tall beer can lying on its side. The lid lifts up like the top of a barbecue grill. Inside is the man who drank two six-packs of the stuff every night while watching sports on his five-hundred-channel satellite dish. What could be more fitting, more touching, more appropriate?

A college football fan could get a coffin in the school colors. The inside would be full of pennants and memorabilia. He'd be supporting his team and easing his way into the hereafter at the same time. The Martha Stewart line of coffins would come in pastels with matching trim. Inside there would be an eiderdown pillow covered with a linen case and lined in the most tasteful white-on-white taffeta. The NASCAR model would come complete with STP and Napa Auto Parts decals. You could pick the number of your favorite driver. Why stop there? You've seen those new headstones with a photo of the deceased engraved on them? Why not a sponsor's name as well? Say a normal headstone is three thousand dollars. Have the words "Got Milk?" on it with a picture of our late friend wearing a milk mustache and the price may drop to fifteen hundred. Tombs in the shape of bowling trophies could be very popular. Me, I'd like to be laid to rest under a large two-foot-high golf ball. On one side it would have my name and dates, on the other "Titleist." Instead of putting housing developments around golf courses, wouldn't it be more practical to put cemeteries around them? No worries about broken windows, no dings in the siding. Besides, I'd get more visitors from other golfers than I ever would from my family. And, like me, I'd know my visitors can't hit the fairway, either.

Lord of the Earrings

After attending a neighborhood picnic the other day I had to ask myself—Will I be the last man in this country to wear a goatee? Will I be the last guy on the planet to get a tattoo? Will I be the last overweight man on the planet to buy a motorcycle? Will I be the last man on my block to wear an earring? And will it go with my hearing aid? Or do they make hearing aids now that look like earrings?

I am so out of it, I don't even know where to go to get my ears pierced. To that booth in the middle of the mall that all the sixth grade girls go to? I'd be so embarrassed if I ran into someone I knew.

"Hey, Jim! How you doing? I haven't seen you since you shaved your head and grew the goatee. That's a nice look for you—if you ever take up professional wrestling. Do they have a senior tour on the WWF?"

And what kind of earrings would I buy? And how many? I see a lot of guys wear diamond studs. Other guys have two little gold hoops on the same ear. Can you have a diamond on one side and a hoop on the other?

I don't know the first thing about jewelry. What if getting an earring doesn't make me look more macho but makes me look less macho? My macho cushion is not that thick. The wrong earring might send a message I don't want to send. Instead of saying "When you see me coming better step aside," it might say, "Let me hold your purse while you go shopping for fabric remnants."

How do I shave a goatee? I'm not that artistic. The two sides won't match. It would take forever. Call me crazy, but I want to spend less time in the bathroom, not more. And my beard color doesn't match my hair color. My hair is salt and pepper (if you use that popular grey pepper) but my beard is salt, pepper, salt and more salt. Would an earring go with that?

Should I shave my head or go with that Johnny Depp *Pirates of the Caribbean* look? I could weave my car keys and reading glasses into my hair extensions so I would never lose them again and look dangerous and out of control at the same time—except for the tie and sport coat.

How do you pick a tattoo? Do you get references?

"Are you the guy that did Melissa's tattoo? Nice work. It looks just like her ex-boyfriend. It's really lifelike. Did you know he's grown a goatee since they broke up? Maybe she'll come in for a touch-up."

And what would my tattoo say? "Mom"? My Mom would have hated that. Or maybe one of those things that look like razor wire circling my bicep. Oh yeah, I don't have much of a bicep. A tattoo will only bring attention to it.

Would I tell Sue before I got my ears pierced? Before I got a tattoo, before I shaved my head and grew a goatee? Hell, no. Why should I? I'm a grown person, I don't need anyone's permission, she's not the boss of me! That's the whole point of the earring—it screams, "You can't tell me what to do! I'm an outlaw, I live by my own rules." And besides, all the other guys have them.

But if I just do it without telling her first, she'll kill me. "Outlaw Renegade Macho Man Kicked Out of House by Tiny Woman" is not a headline I want to read.

When You Care Enough to Write Your Very Own

When an elderly neighbor we barely knew died recently I went to the drug store to buy a sympathy card to send to his wife. I was looking for something sober and simple. A plain white card that said something like, "We were saddened to hear of your loss. Please accept our sincere condolences. Our thoughts are with you at this sad time."

That, you cannot buy. You can, however, buy any number of cards with embossed silver lilies on the front that say, with small variations, "He was the best person on Earth and after he invented cold fusion and time travel he gave all his money to widows and orphans. When he wasn't feeding the homeless, he was building them houses. Albert Schweitzer and Mother Teresa wished they were as good and kind as he was. I beg you to make it a closed coffin funeral or I might jump in. Why him, Lord, and not me?"

That was more than I really wanted to say. Maybe someone closer to him, say, the oil delivery guy or his septic tank cleaner, could send something that flowery, but I was practically a stranger. Besides, it was so vague, like one of those eulogies by a preacher who never met the deceased. I've been to funerals when after the preacher's finished I take a second look at the program to make sure we're burying the right person. If that card was too flowery, others were not flowery enough. I didn't have the heart to put my signature on this one either:

"Even though he was in a nursing home for the last eight years and hadn't spoken in six, we were shocked. We'd been planning to go see him for years and now it's too late. If only he could have hung on until our kids finished soccer season, we could have been there for him. If you need anything, I mean anything, please let us know. Well, not on Tuesdays, that's Jim's bowling night. And Fridays are pretty bad, too. Sue's taking that Thai cooking class. What's going to happen to that big roll top desk he had? It would really look good in our library. I'm sorry, that was an insensitive thing to say. You might think it will look better in our family room. Who are we to tell you what to do? Thursdays are no good at all. That's *Survivor* night. We never miss it. Now that I think about it, you're the one with all the free time now. Maybe you should come over here and help *us*. They say work will take your mind off your troubles."

While looking for something with just the right tone, I accidentally picked up some cards from the "Birthday—Seniors" section. "Hey, you old geezer, drop dead and make room on the planet for someone else," read the first one. "I wanted to get you something extra special, but Dr. Kevorkian is in jail," said the second. "I gave you this same card last year, but you probably can't remember it, can you, you senile old fool?" said the third. I'm starting to think that what carried my neighbor off might have been a torrent of brutal birthday cards.

I wonder if the cards are having the opposite effect of what is intended. Instead of saying "We're thinking about you," they may be saying "This is all the time I'm willing to waste on you." One card company has a slo-gan, "When you care enough to send the very best." They're right. I did what I should have done from the start and wrote a note to the new widow on my own sta-tionery. Weeks later she told me it was the only hand-written note she'd received.

Dude, Where's My Horse?

Hey, pardner, when you've had enough of the hustle and bustle of city life, it's time to visit the Lazy A Hole Ranch in the heart of the pristine, unspoiled, uncrowded, undiscovered Mosquito Grande Mountains.

Not for tenderfeet, the Lazy A Hole is that real cowboy experience you've been looking for. Imagine getting up with the sun after sleeping under the stars. Imagine brushing off spiders and centipedes as you crawl behind the nearest tree to use our huge, spacious, open-air, pine-scented bathrooms.

The Lazy A is not only fun, it's educational! You'll learn how to identify crawling, flying, and stinging insects, a wide variety of nocturnal rodents and multiple bird droppings up close and personal-like. You'll learn by actually touching them which plants will sting and cut and which ones won't; you'll learn which ones will leave a nasty rash. No need for book learning and memorization here. Once you've spent an evening pulling burrs out of your underwear, you won't never forget what purple thistle looks like.

Then Cookie will serve you a real cowhand's breakfast—blackened eggs, blackened toast, blackened bacon, blackened home fries, blackened orange juice. From roadkill to free-range beef, there's practically nothing he can't blacken, and you'll wash all of it down with his blackened coffee. None of your citified, fancy-schmanzy latte grandes out here, no sirree.

No fancy-schmanzy city doctors, either. Rope burn? See Cookie. Dislocated shoulder? See Cookie. Snake bite? See Cookie. Broken bone stickin' through your skin? See Cookie. He's got a wide variety of ointments and folk remedies that have kept our ranch hands on the job for years past their due date. Just ask One-Eye Pete, One-Arm Dave, or me, Coughin' Bob: would we rather go to a doctor or just see Cookie? True, we did lose One-Ear Joe in an unfortunate branding iron accident but that 'twere mostly his own fault.

At the Lazy A, you'll be doin' the job of a real, honest-to-God cowpoke—mine. I ain't been able to do much since I caught that horseshoe in the head. Cookie puts a stinging poultice on it once a week made out of ground up lightning bugs and axle grease, but there are some things modern medicine can't yet fix. You'll cut cattle, stack hay, feed the calves, clean the barn, and mend fence in the heat and in the pouring rain, all the time waving and slapping at black flies, gnats, and mosquitoes as big as your boot.

And don't ignore the health benefits of the great outdoors. Some spas charge you thousands of dollars a week to take a few mudbaths and to lose a few pounds. At the Lazy A you'll get more exercise in one afternoon slapping away no-see-um bugs than you'll ever get at some high-faluting air-conditioned health spa. Mud bath? By the end of a Lazy A day you'll get covered in filth nature's way, on the back of a horse.

You'll feel the calories burn away after fourteen hours on the back of a sweaty horse in the blazin' sun. Hell, if you don't get skin cancer by the end of the week, we ain't been doin' our job. 'Course you won't be gettin' it on your inner thigh, 'cause that skin'll all be gone by the end of the first day. When it comes to losing ugly pounds, Cookie's food puts the Atkins, the Zone, and Sugar Busters diets to shame. I've been losing ten pounds a year right steady. I'm down to 130. I can get my whole body in one of my old pant legs.

But the most important thing is the memories you'll have for the rest of your life: discovering you've bedded down on top of a fire ant's nest; nearly getting washed away in a flash flood; catching your pant leg on fire and having your new ranch friends stomp it out for you.

If this sounds like the life you've always dreamt of having but never did, give us a call. It's only $2,750 a week. Plus tax and tips. For $2,850 a week I'll let you do my laundry, too.

Not-so-natural Disasters

Animals can sense it coming long before the humans. The cats run and hide; the cows in fields stop chewing and turn their heads; flocks of crows fly out of the trees; the deer feasting in Sue's garden bolt. They know something very bad is about to happen: an earthquake, a tornado, a tsunami. We humans miss the signs; we sit here until it is almost upon us but even *we* can hear this before we see it. Suddenly it appears. It makes the turn right onto our dirt road and heads straight at us. The concussion waves are so powerful dishes start to shake and the plaster rattles. It is a 2001 blue Chevy compact driven by Spike, the nineteen-year-old son of one of the neighbors. To call it a car is silly. It is a giant speaker on wheels.

Spike's head smacks the back of the headrest over and over as he drives past us. The only sound that escapes the car is a booty-shaking bass. What must it sound like inside that tiny car? The sound may be so powerful in such an enclosed space that his chromosomes may actually split apart, making it impossible for him to father children. So there could be an upside.

We are eighty miles in any direction from what anyone could properly call a city. We live on a dead end road, there are only five houses on the road past ours, and the space is so vast you can't see one house from the other. How could you possibly get more peace and quiet?

By living on a NASCAR track, that's how.

Spike listens to gangsta rap. There are very few gangstas in our little town of twenty-five hundred people. There is the guy who got arrested for stealing the large capstones from old stone fences and using them to build a backyard patio. And there was the obstetrician who left his wife and ran off with a nurse. And Monday's paper always lists a few DUI violations but I'm pretty sure that's not the kind of crime that gives you the street cred that Lil Wayne and 50 Cent are rapping about.

Besides, Sue and I know Spike; we know he's not a problem kid. He calls me "Sir" and her "Ma'am." He's about as scary as a Muppet. You couldn't meet a nicer, more polite young man.

That's why we feel so bad about wanting to have him killed. We have long discussions on our front porch about how to make it look like an accident. A gun seems so, well, traceable. Poison mushrooms, too imprecise. He may hate mushrooms and the rest of his family may like them. Tamper with his brakes? He might hit our house. Tie him up in the basement and make him watch *The Sound of Music* over and over? Please, we're not that inhuman. Still, we watch *CSI* now hoping against hope to find a murder that even they can't solve.

He makes ten or twenty trips a day, spreading his musical message. He needs a job, that would solve his problem and ours. So we made a few phone calls. Today a new car made a trip up and down the road. It was the Army recruiter Sue called to give Spike's name and address.

Is Our Children Learning?

Welcome back, class. I hope you all completed your Spring Break reading assignments, *Who Moved My Cheese* and *The South Beach Diet*. We'll be discussing those and the other classics during English Lit this semester. We'll try to get through *The Secret* before the ten-day "Pre-Summer-Holiday Student-Stress-Relief Break" which starts in one week.

There has been a change in the History curriculum: we'll be studying the third season of *Glee* this year, not the second as it says in your printed class schedule. In the two weeks between the Pre-Summer Holiday and the April break we will be covering *That 70s Show* so if you haven't been watching that, you'd better get started. There will be a quiz on the fashions of the '70s as well as the decor.

Those of you who had Mr. Grunion for remedial Tivoing last semester should know what he did on his Spring Break. I suppose the easiest way to explain it is that he's Miss Grunion now, and in addition to Tivo, she will be coaching the girls' softball team. Go Redheads! As you know, the Redheads had a dismal one-and-fourteen season last year and Miss Grunion thinks they're capable of doing much better. At least twice as well, she promises. Still, they did capture the "Courage to Show Up" Cup, which is displayed in the trophy case in the main hall. Two more of those and we will have more of them than any other high school in the state.

The school board has made a few rule changes, so listen up. All tattoos must be tasteful and PG-13. No swear words without a parent or guardian's permission, especially on the fingers. There will be a limit of three piercings per face, excluding the ears. That is, you could have one eyebrow, one lip and one nose pierced, or two eyebrows and one nose, but you can't have two eyebrows, a nose, and a lip. Is that understood?

It sounds harsh, but these rules are for your own protection. We had several painful and ugly accidents last year and no one wants a repeat of that. I think that sight of Billy Chambers stuck to the tennis court fence will haunt me for the rest of my life. They say his nose reattachment went well, but he still hasn't returned to class.

As you all know, thongs must be worn *inside* your clothes. What you do at home is your own business, but here at school we have standards. There will be no online shopping allowed this year during school hours. Those laptops are for studying, people, not shopping. And don't bother to try. We've worked out a deal with FedEx—they will no longer deliver packages to this school except to teachers and administrators. Is that clear?

Between the Post-Christmas Holidays and the Pre-Midwinter Rest we've added a teacher's conference. So there are only ten school days between December 15th and April 5th and we will have to cram in a lot of work.

Sit down, Mr. Wilson. The mid-morning snack bell hasn't rung yet. The Starbucks will still be in the cafeteria when the bell rings. Which reminds me: those of you who have signed up for "Cell Phone Plan Management," would you please raise your hands? That's not many. I know it's the toughest course we offer, but you really should think about taking it. It will stretch your minds and save you money. There's the bell. Remember, you've only got an hour snack this year, so try not to be late for your next class.

Why Isn't this Man Running the World?

There is a man who knows how to solve all the problems in the Middle East quickly and easily. He knows exactly what we should do in Iraq. He has the solution to global climate change, the high price of gas, the immigration turmoil, affirmative action, stem cell research, gangs, and the drug problem.

He can speak extemporaneously for hours on tax fairness, campaign finance reform, universal health care, voter fraud, education reform, farm subsidies, and foreign aid.

Nothing is too big or too small to escape his notice. In the past half hour he has touched on Indian casinos, the crisis in Darfur, Al Gore, Rosie O'Donnell, globalization, spice rubs, and the iPhone.

And where is this man? Teaching at one of the great universities? Writing position papers for some prestigious think tank? In the executive suite of a multinational corporation? Out on the campaign trail running for office?

No, he's right at the table next to us at the Big Pig restaurant. What luck! Not only is he an expert on world and national affairs, he is extremely principled and highly moral. He has nothing but contempt for athletes who take steroids or athletes who don't win one hundred percent of the time. They are miserable, despicable failures who lack character. They are bad role models who corrupt our youth by sending out the wrong message about hard work and dedication.

Worse, they screw up his betting system. Which is why, through absolutely no fault of his own, he's three years behind on his child support, because of all those lazy, good-for-nothing, overpaid athletes.

The overpaid athletes rank right up there with the overpaid Hollywood celebrities who change partners faster than you can change channels on your TV. Their marriages fail because they are so self-centered and egotistical.

They can't think past themselves. Whereas his own three marriages failed because his wives were all nagging witches. Nag, nag, nag—Nagging him to get a job, nagging him to stop drinking, nagging him to take a shower, nagging him to fix the car so she could drive to work instead of walking to the bus.

"The walking would have done her good. Get some pounds off her butt."

So, it's not just world and national affairs that he's an expert on, he is also an expert on women, most of whom do not come up to his high standards of height-weight proportion, gymnastic ability, and buttock size.

That restraining order that his second ex-wife has taken out on him that says he can't come within a thousand yards of her or the kids is based on a complete misunderstanding. He was simply cleaning the baseball bat when it slipped from his hands and accidentally destroyed the dinette set in the kitchen and her collection of Lladro figurines in the living room.

Now, because of her, his children will be deprived of a father's tender love. How will they learn how to fish? To hunt? To cheat on their taxes? To hotwire a car? To post bail? To drive on a suspended license? Who will teach them that? An overpaid, morally-deficient judge?

As we ate dessert, we learned how to solve our problems with North Korea, our trade deficit with China, oil drilling, and the crystal meth epidemic. Finally he left and we got to pay our bill in delightful silence.

"This guy can't even run his own life but he thinks he should be running the world," I said to Sue.

"What makes you think he isn't?" she asked.

Merry Christmas, Inc.

The Christmas card from our bank is on the mantel with all the other Christmas cards: the ones from the credit card companies, the one from the auto dealer, the one from the mortgage company, the ones from the charities we stopped giving money to fifteen years ago, the one from our senator, the one from our congressman, the one from a hotel chain we stayed at once, the one from Recliner City, and the one from our cell phone provider. Yet they say no one has the Christmas spirit any more.

I thought my mortgage company was your typical cold, hard-hearted, bottom-line conglomerate, and then we received this bright red and gold Christmas card that says "From your friends at First Financial." How I misjudged them. It turns out I have many dear, close friends there. Why there's what's-her-face and what's-his-name—that guy with the toupee—Bob or Charlie or Pete or something. I don't know why we've never had them over for dinner. Maybe it's because we've had no contact with them whatsoever in the six years since the closing. Who could miss the personalized seasonal message they put on the bulk rate meter stamp: "Can You Save Money by Refinancing this Season?"

Our auto dealer's card had a picture of all their salesmen wearing Santa hats gathered around their latest, shiny, fire-engine-red sports car. "'Tis the Season to drop in and test drive the brand-new Labrador. It's big and friendly and loves attention! Buy one today! From Santa's Helpers at the New and Used Auto Warehouse!" It was addressed to "Resident." It made me feel all warm and fuzzy inside to know they're full of the Christmas spirit. I guess we have to send them a card now. We got one from the Tire Barn, too. Better add them to the list.

Our stockbroker sent us two cards, one for my 401k and one for my regular account. That's so thoughtful. How does he remember? He must have a brain like a computer. And such an expensive-looking card. Five dollars apiece, I would think. I wonder where he gets all the money? The broker's card covers all the holiday bases; it says "Happy Holidays," "Merry Christmas," "Happy Hanukkah," "Feliz Navidad," "Joyeux Noel," "Kwanzaa Yenu Iwe Na Heri," and "Gajan Kristnaskon." His pagan customers must be miffed that there's no "Have a Festive Saturnalia," but you can't please everyone.

I do a lot of business online, so I get a lot of online Christmas cards from people who have my credit card number and my e-mail address. It's becoming a long list. Should I print out their cards or just leave them on the computer? Some of them sing and dance. Don't you love it when you're supposed to be hard at work and you open an e-mail and then, at double the volume of anything else going on in the office a bunch of barking dogs start singing "Jingle Bells?" My boss had the bonus envelopes in his hand when that happened. Now I'll never know what mine would have been.

I do get a lot of cards from old friends and far-flung family members, but they rarely contain any coupons or an offer for a free, three-day visit to a time-share like the cards my corporate friends send me, or ten percent off last Christmas's hot toy. I want to call up my cheap relatives and say, "Hey, what's the matter with you? Don't you know the true meaning of Christmas? I'm taking you off my Christmas card list," but then I calm down and ask myself, "What would my big box store do?" They never take *anyone* off their Christmas card list.

Spare the Taser, Spoil the Child

There was a huge crash from the living room. A second later New Hampshire skated through the kitchen on his Heelys screaming "Watch me! Watch me!" as he slammed into our refrigerator.

New Hampshire is my cousin's six-year-old. He won't eat vegetables, and is allergic to gluten, peanuts, latex, penicillin, cats, bees and shellfish. He is, against all odds, overweight. And surly. I can't tell you how much I look forward to their visits.

His parents, Hanna and Pat, had their hearts set on naming him after a state like Indiana Jones but all the good state names were gone by the time he was born. In New Hampshire's first grade class there are two Dakotas, two Nevadas, a Montana, a Georgia, a Florida, a Virginia, a Tennessee, and an Arizona. Hanna thought New Mexico sounded too Latin, Massachusetts sounded too WASPy, and Oregon was too California. Pat confuses Iowa, Idaho, and Ohio, so those were out. All in all, the kid's lucky he's not going through life named American Samoa or Dry Tortuga.

There was some worry what nickname his classmates and friends would give him: "New" or "Hamps" or something strange or rude. They need not have worried. The kid cannot possibly have any friends. His sister Chardonnay has let it slip that several teachers threatened to put him in "the hole. Whatever that is." I'll have to rent *The Great Escape* for her someday.

"What was that crash?" Sue asked.

"It wasn't me," New Hampshire said before Sue had even finished the question. "It just fell over all by itself."

"What fell over by itself?"

"That big stupid red thing."

"That big stupid red vase we got on our honeymoon in Venice thirty-two years ago? That big stupid red thing?"

"Ye-ah, I guess."

Sue and I said nothing as we waited for the parenting to begin.

"New Hampshire is an Indigo Child," Hanna said as New Hampshire skated as fast as he could toward me and, at the last moment, kicked me as hard as he could in the knee. He giggled and then tried to kick me again.

"I'm sorry. We had no idea. Is there a cure?"

Hanna and Pat and New Hampshire all burst out laughing. "A cure? I hope not. New Hampshire has evolved. He's the next step on the evolutionary ladder. A smarter, better human."

"You're saying he's not human?"

"We don't let non-humans play in the house," said Sue. "Or skate," pushing New Hampshire out the back door. "Can he sleep outside?"

"It's not a disease, it's evolution. He's evolved past us the same way we evolved past the Neanderthals. That's why people have a hard time understanding him." Hanna carefully explained to us that Indigo Children don't like to follow rules, they have trouble waiting in line, they are very demanding and insist that they be served first because they know they are special. "He's on a totally different plane than we are. To him, you and I are little more than cats and dogs that can talk, that's how advanced he is."

"We had a word for children like that when I was growing up," Sue said. "But it wasn't 'Indigo.' It was . . ."

"I know, I know, but New Hampshire is beyond 'gifted.' Indigo Children are very intelligent. They also tend to be hyperactive and aggressive."

"Why do they call them Indigo Children instead of. . . ?" Sue asked.

Hanna interrupted again.

"They're Indigo Children because you can see their auras. They can see the future."

"You mean he can predict what he's going to break even before he breaks it? That *is* amazing."

"New Hampshire has evolved past material things. They mean nothing to him. All we can do is watch and admire him."

"I wish you had mentioned this Indigo Child thing before. Our house isn't really advanced being-proofed. We don't have any furniture that won't break when he jumps up and down on it, or the kind of pottery that doesn't break when he runs through the house at a hundred miles an hour like his hair is on fire. Or can he fix the things he breaks with his superpowers?"

"No, not yet, but that may come," said Hanna. "Right now we just have to learn to live with it."

"Are there any other Indigo Children in his school, other kids like him?" Sue asked.

"Oh, yes," said Hanna. "Practically all of them."

American Idol—
1962 Edition

RYAN SEACREST: First up is a singer and guitar player from Hibbing, Minnesota, who calls himself Bob Dylan. We wanted all the contestants to sing Bobby Vee songs tonight, but here's a guy who goes his own way and would rather play something he wrote himself. Very risky. What are you going to do for us tonight, Bobby?

BOB DYLAN: Don't call me Bobby. I'm a grown man. I'm going to do a song called "Desolation Row."

RYAN SEACREST: Wow! What a downer. All right, Bob, give it your best shot.

BOB SINGS.

RYAN SEACREST: So Judges, what did you think? Randy?

RANDY JACKSON: Yo, dog, what's up? I have to tell you man, that didn't do it for me. You were a little pitchy all through the thing. And folk music? That's a fad, man. How long's that going to last?

PAULA ABDUL: That was the best thing I've ever heard. You're going all the way to the top.

SIMON COWELL: I have to be honest with you, Bob. Who told you you could sing? And that song. What a poor choice. Couldn't you pick a Four Freshmen song or a Lettermen song or at least a Jimmy Dean song?

RYAN SEACREST: So there you have it from the judges, Bob, what did you think about your performance?

BOB DYLAN: You got a lot of nerve, to say you are my friend.

RYAN SEACREST: Thank you, Bob. If you want to vote for Bob Dylan, the number to call is PLaza one one one.

Next up is a singer from Port Arthur, Texas named Janis Joplin. Janis said she'd sing a Bobby Vee song when pigs fly. She'll be performing the

Gershwin classic "Summertime" from *Porgy and Bess*.

JOPLIN SINGS.

RYAN SEACREST: Well, that was—different. Judges, what have you got to say?

RANDY JACKSON: Yo, what's up dog?

JANIS: Who are you calling a dog? You call me that one more time and I'll come over there and smack you. Don't think I won't.

RANDY: I don't know what to say. Do you have a cold? Tuberculosis? You should see a doctor about that. Let me tell you, that's not the way Shelley Fabares would have done that song.

PAULA ABDUL: That was the best thing I've ever heard. You're going all the way to the top.

SIMON COWELL: I don't know what to say. That is the worst performance I've ever heard. By a human. It sounded like two cats fighting in a burlap bag. The only reason you won't be voted off tonight is because that Bob Dylan guy was worse.

RYAN SEACREST: Oh, that was bitter. What did you think of your performance tonight, Janis?

JANIS: What are you guys looking for? A singer or Playmate of the Month?

RYAN SEACREST: Janis Joplin, ladies and gentlemen! The audience at home can vote for her by dialing PLaza two two two.

Now a young singer from London, England, Mick Jagger. He, too, has refused to sing a Bobby Vee song and will be performing "Route 66."

MICK SINGS.

RYAN SEACREST: Quite the little dancer, aren't you. OK, judges, let's see what you thought about Mick's performance. Randy?

RANDY JACKSON: What's up, dog? First of all, you're not American. I don't know how you got through the door in the first place. Second, what is all that stuff with the hands and the hips? Are you singing or trying to charm snakes?

PAULA ABDUL: That was the best thing I've ever heard. You're going all the way to the top.

SIMON COWELL: Mick, Mick, Mick. I'm not trying to be rude here, but let me just tell you there is no way you're ever going to make it in this business. First, that accent, and second, look at you. Long hair on men? That went out in 1776. Are you wearing lipstick? I'm sorry, but you're just not American Idol potential.

RYAN SEACREST: There you have it from the judges. If you'd like to vote for Mick Jagger dial PLaza three three three. After the break we'll come back with three more contestants: Bobby Goldsboro, Bobby Rydell and a Singing Nun. Stay tuned!

The Only
Possible Explanation

Do not throw this letter away. Todd B. of Chillecothe, Ohio got this letter a year and a half ago and he threw it away. He thought THE CHAIN was a joke. He lost all the money in his retirement account and his house is in foreclosure. Believe in the power of THE CHAIN. Don't break THE CHAIN.

The executives of Goldman Sachs, AIG, and a bunch of other banks got this letter in late 2008 and each one sent it to twenty congressmen. They made billions. And they were rich to begin with! THE CHAIN is strong! Believe in the power of THE CHAIN.

Robin C. of Culpepper, Virginia got this letter and thought it was a scam from his ex-sister-in-law so he threw it away. He did not send it to twenty of his friends. He lost his job and his benefits. His boss sent this letter to all the board members that he appointed. He got a six-million-dollar bonus even though the company he ran lost money and their stock is in the toilet! He believed in the Power of THE CHAIN! Don't break THE CHAIN; the Power of THE CHAIN is strong!

Melvin T. of Manatee, Florida got this letter, but since he had invested wisely in a balanced portfolio of stocks recommended by the experts on the financial news channels, he burned the letter in his poolside barbeque while his friends watched and laughed. Melvin was wiped out. His wife left him and his children had to leave college because he couldn't pay their tuition. All the financial TV experts sent the letter to twenty of their friends in the media. They all got big raises. Don't break THE CHAIN, the Power of THE CHAIN is strong!

Lois L. works for a big insurance company in their "Denying Claims" call center. Her company makes a lot of money, but she doesn't. None of her co-workers makes a lot of money, either. She's very tired at the end of the day from explaining to people what a pre-existing condition means. She and her husband are raising three kids. Lois and her husband discussed joining THE CHAIN, but they fell asleep from overwork and the next day they had a teacher's conference with little Billy's teacher. They forgot about the power of THE CHAIN. The company did not have enough money to give Lois the raise she asked for. Her co-pay has gone up fifty percent; her deductible is now $2,500 a year.

The CEO that runs the insurance company Lois works for had one of his secretaries mail the letter to 20 lobbyists. He paid himself over forty million dollars last year. The company pays for his corporate jet and his golf and ski club memberships. The Power of THE CHAIN is strong. Don't break THE CHAIN.

THE CHAIN is getting sick of all you poor people ignoring the chain. Get with the program, would you? THE CHAIN helps those that help themselves. All the Chrysler and GM executives got THE CHAIN and sent it to twenty of their friends. They know the power of THE CHAIN. That's how they all got their jobs in the first place. Trust THE CHAIN. THE CHAIN is strong. Believe in the power of THE CHAIN!

Let Me Hear
Your Body Talk

Spoiler Alert! If you haven't had a colonoscopy yet, don't read any further, I don't want you to miss all the fun. First of all, everyone at the hospital is happy to see you, because forty percent of the people scheduled for colonoscopies don't show up. The doctor was amazingly cheerful as he told me he'd never perforated anyone's colon yet, but there was a one-in-five-thousand chance he would.

"How many colonoscopies have you done?"

"4,999. Now if you could just sign this form that says I told you about the one-in-five-thousand chance, we can give you something that will relax you and I'll go to work."

The guy sticking electrode clips to my chest couldn't have been happier. The nurse who put a toasted hot flannel blanket over me also seemed oddly happy. Me, all I could think about was, please finish this so I can run out of here and get something to eat. I'd been on special diets for a week—don't eat this, don't eat that, two days before only liquids, one day before only clear liquids. Drink this awful stuff and take these pills the night before. When I got to the clinic, the form asked me if I had taken all the Miralax and the Dulcolax that had been prescribed. I checked "yes." The next question was, "What were the results?"

It's impossible to put down the results on the one-inch-long blank space that was on the form. There wasn't enough room to say, "I got no sleep at all due to the fact that I had to run to the bathroom once an hour on the hour for twelve hours. Several times I got there with just seconds to spare. I am seven pounds lighter than I was yesterday and my stomach is queasy. I haven't had any fruit or vegetables in five days and I may never eat chicken consommé again." What were the results? I wrote, "About what you'd expect."

Compared to that last night, the colonoscopy was a picnic. It only took about fifteen minutes, it was painless and it turns out that I have the colon of a sixteen-year-old—a big, fat, out-of-shape sixteen-year-old. The doctor handed me a summary of the procedure with color pictures of my colon included.

"Do you want me to e-mail them to your friends and family?"

"Gee, thanks, but I'll just post them on my Facebook page when I get home."

There was one little thing they forgot to mention about the procedure.

"The doctor pumps air in your colon as they do the colonoscopy to open it up. That air will cause discomfort until you let it out," Nurse Happy told me.

"What do you mean, let it out?"

"Don't hold it in, let it out."

I'm lying in bed in some kind of recovery room with about twenty other people within whispering distance. "You mean . . ."

"Yeah," she tells me. "We can't let you go until you let it out."

Call me repressed, but there are certain things I cannot do in public—dance, drink, floss, spit, talk on a cell phone—up to and including letting it out. Because of the drugs, after about ten minutes I told her I had let it out. Because of the drugs, they insisted that Sue drive me home. Because of the drugs, I insisted that we stop at a family-style restaurant on the way so I could eat some real food for the first time in a week. I ordered everything and wolfed it down. What happened next was, well, about what you'd expect. That was the most painful part of the whole procedure: being banned from Applebee's for life.

Not Even My
Best Friends Know

L ike millions of people around the world, I strug-
gle with a severe learning disability. It often
causes me to say things that I regret, it wreaks
emotional and financial damage on my friends and family, and it has cost my employers tens of thousands of
dollars over the years.

It's not one of those trendy conditions that everybody
and their brother has, like ADD or ADHD or even
AADD. It's not something all the movie stars brag about
having, like dyslexia. It's an embarrassing and rarely-
mentioned disorder that I have long kept secret, afraid
my friends, my neighbors, and my co-workers would dis-
cover it and make me an object of scorn and ridicule. But

now is the time to come out of the closet—I suffer from
. . . Stupidity.

No one brags about the heartbreak of Stupidity. There's
no pill you can take for it, there's no support group, no
summer camp especially for us. You just have to learn to
live with it. Parents that have no problem telling the world
their child has ADD or ADHD wouldn't be caught dead
standing up at a PTA meeting and saying, "My kid's just
plain stupid. Got any special programs for that?"

Even in this modern day and age, Stupidity still carries
a stigma with it—some people even believe that stupid
people aren't quite as good as "normal" people—even
though we've had stupid presidents, stupid socialites,
stupid generals, stupid movie stars, stupid bankers and
stupid CEOs. Stupidity knows no borders. Many people
suffer from Stupidity and don't even know it. My friend
Sal thinks the Presidents' faces on Mount Rushmore
were carved by the wind. Yet he holds a good-paying job
and has a family. His wife and many of his children are
non-stupid.

Stupidity has never become a fashionable disorder.
None of the morning show hosts have ever done a

weeklong series on it; none of them have admitted to having raised C-minus children.

Little is known about stupidity even though scientists say that statistically, as much as half of the entire population of the planet is below average. An exaggeration, no doubt. Stupidity is an equal-opportunity disability, striking both men and women, the young and old, teachers and students, princes and paupers, politicians and voters, athletes and, well, a whole lot of athletes.

Stupidity can strike without warning. Who hasn't married someone and then smacked his or her forehead ten minutes later and said, "What was I thinking?" What CEO hasn't paid him or herself a hundred million dollars and then fired a thousand people in a cost-cutting measure?

An especially tragic form of the disease is Adult Onset Stupidity (AOS). One day you're perfectly normal and healthy, the next day you're watching TV shows about bass fishing.

For years, I hid my Stupidity from my friends, my family and my co-workers. Only my wife knew about it, which is amazing, because I never told her I had it; she figured it out all by herself. It used to bother me, but now, when I come home from the grocery store and she yells, "You idiot, I said 'tuna fish,' not 'Tidy Flush!'" I don't take it personally. Instead of hiding my stupidity from her, I can relax at home and be as stupid as I like. She won't let me cook or clean or do the laundry because I always "do it wrong." While she does the dishes, I watch TV. Sometimes I think, "Who's stupid, now?" But I don't say it out loud. I'm not *that* stupid.

Over the years, I've gotten good at finding ways to hide my Stupidity from others. When I misspelled the company's name on this year's Christmas cards, I blamed the stupid printers. When I bought the lead paint for the company's Day Care Center because it was on sale, I blamed the stupid paint store. When I forget to mail things out—important things like bills and contracts—I blame the Post Office. My bosses always blame other people, so I figure it's the smart thing to do. I don't want them to think I'm stupid.

That Crazy Little Thing
Called "That Thing"

"Sore throat?"

"Yes."

"Coughing?"

"Yes."

"Can't sleep?"

"That's it."

"Feel tired and cranky?"

"Yes, dammit!"

Stan, in his long white jacket, nods knowingly. He already has seen many, many cases like mine this morning. If only he were a doctor and not my butcher I would feel better. "It's the same thing Bob has," he pronounces. With no urine sample, no chest X-ray, no stethoscope,

Stan the butcher has done what Ben Casey couldn't. Would Stan be offended if I got a second opinion from the guy down at H & R Block who does my taxes?

"It's your life," says Stan. "If you want to throw it away on some quack, be my guest. He'll tell you the same thing, it'll just cost you more."

"For once Stan is right," says Charlie the tax preparer. "You've got the same thing Bob has. We're seeing a lot of that this year. But I can't believe you went to Stan before you came to me. Stan's an idiot. He tried to do his own taxes one year. He took deductions even Willie Nelson wouldn't try to get away with. When are you guys ever going to learn?"

"So that's the diagnosis? I have that thing that's going around? How long does it last?"

"We don't know. Bob's still got it. It's been almost a month."

"He's still got it? But he was at our house for dinner just last Sunday. Don't you think Bob should stay away from people until he's feeling better? Do you really think it's smart for him to go out while he's still sick?" Was Typhoid Bob going around town spreading this on purpose?

Didn't this thing hit me Monday or Tuesday, right after we saw him?

Julie, the high school French teacher, also thought I might have that thing that's going around.

"Drink plenty of fluids and watch *The Young and the Restless*," she told me.

"Why should I watch *The Young and the Restless*?"

"You don't have to, but it always makes me feel better. No matter how bad things are going in my life, I can always be sure that it's going worse for the people on that show."

It's sad that despite all the advances we've made in butchering, accounting, and French lessons over the years, there is still no cure for that thing that's going around. What's worse, I'm not really sure Stan, Charlie, and Julie are even *working* on a cure.

I suppose I could go to a real doctor and sit around a waiting room full of coughing, sneezing, sick people, but I'm afraid I'll catch something new. If I start drinking green tea and taking echinacea it should go away. Or should I try Western medicine? We've got plenty of that lying around the house.

At the bottom of the bathroom drawer I found three foil-backed sheets of pills, half used, each sheet with pills a different color. There were no instructions, no clue as to exactly what they were supposed to cure. Were these for allergies or for nasal congestion? Or were they for those achy, flu-like symptoms? Is this an anti-histamine? What is histamine, anyway, and should I be against it? What if I'm pro-histamine? I also found many half-used bottles of various cough medicines, some for daytime, some for night. They all said not to drive while taking the stuff because it will make you drowsy. Not drowsy enough to sleep, just drowsy enough so that you can't drive. After a couple of drowsy but sleepless cough-filled nights, it finally hits me that maybe I should try sleeping in my car.

Sue had made that very same suggestion days ago. She doesn't really care if I get any sleep, she just doesn't want to catch that thing that's going around.

Office Memo
Re: Girl Scout Cookies
To: All Employees

Representatives of my daughter Merlot will be in the office today selling Girl Scout cookies. Of course, no one should feel any pressure to buy from her just because she's the boss's daughter. I know there's a rumor going around that Roberts was fired last year for not placing an order, but it's not true. He was fired for wearing a suit on casual Friday.

When one of Merlot's designated representatives knocks on your cubicle, just pretend it's one of the kids in your neighborhood. After you fill out the order form, Jeanine from my office will collect them, because Merlot has ADD and we don't want a repeat of last year's problems.

I didn't find out until months later that none of you had gotten your cookies. Someone should have told me. It wasn't until Roberts mentioned it that I became aware of the problem and by then it was too late to do anything about it. I asked Merlot what happened and she said, "Whatever. It's just some cookies, what's the big deal?" And then she stomped out of the room.

And that's why selling Girl Scout cookies is such a wonderful thing. It's teaching young women like Merlot life lessons: how to present themselves, how to get along with people, how to get along in the real world, the value of hard work, and how to be an entrepreneur—all the things Merlot knows nothing about and really needs to learn. I'm hoping she will learn when she comes back from Paris and gets a briefing from our department heads on the cookie sales. Merlot had to go to Paris for a second fitting of her Brownie uniform and to pick up some of that perfume she likes, so she won't actually be seeing any of you in person, but she'll know how much you care by how many boxes of cookies you buy.

For the sake of convenience, Merlot is not taking any orders of less than six boxes apiece this year, so let's keep it simple, people. Some of you should just order six boxes of Thin Mints, others six boxes of Shortbread, and others six boxes of Lemon Pastry Cremes and then you can trade amongst yourselves when they arrive. Of course you can order more than six boxes, but who's counting?

Shortly before that ugly casual Friday incident, Roberts said the strangest thing to me. "Wouldn't it be easier if the Girl Scouts just asked me for ten bucks outright instead of trying to get me to buy twenty dollars worth of cookies I don't need and don't want?" he asked. "They wouldn't have to make them and bake them and box them and ship them. They're full of hydrogenated oil and sugar and no one should be eating them, much less pushing them. Then the Girl Scouts wouldn't have to account for them; they wouldn't have to fill out order forms. Why don't we just donate some money to the Girl Scouts and forget the cookies?"

The poor deluded crank. I hope he never has children. Can you imagine how they'd turn out?

I won't waste your time sending Merlot around to say "Thank You" because after all, time is money and I'm not sure we should be wasting time on personal stuff like that, so I'll say "Thank You" for her. But you should thank yourselves, too. Someday, when Merlot is running this company, you can all look at one another and know that you helped teach her all the skills she will need to get ahead in business.

Daddy Dearest

The model in the fancy department store ad looks as if he is eighteen or twenty. His thick blond hair is cut just so, his chiseled chin is tilted slightly down, his tapered body is perfectly proportioned. He probably did a few hundred push-ups while waiting for the photographer's assistant to set up the lights for this particular shot. He is wearing the latest in trendy weekend clothes for the young, rich man—a $350 designer shirt that looks like something Brad Pitt might wear to pitch meetings with Hollywood producers. Casually expensive, hugging his perfect, sculpted body. The ad, of course, is for Father's Day.

It doesn't look like the male model is thinking of his children. It looks more like he's thinking of the Victoria's Secret model that he'll be taking nightclubbing tonight.

Trying to picture my 83-year-old Dad in such an expensive, trendy outfit makes me a tad queasy. Not only would he never speak to me again for spending $350 on a shirt, but it would look ridiculous on him. After a certain age there is no point trying to dress men up. It's like putting clothes on a dog. No one's going to thank you and the dog looks uncomfortable. Besides, Dad's a flannel guy all the way. I would sooner get him to wear opera hose, a black leather lace-up bustier and carry a whip before I'd get him into a $350 designer shirt.

I try to picture other dads I know in this outfit and it doesn't work, either. For some reason they just don't have the time to dote on fashion they way they did before they were fathers. Instead of going to the health club for a couple hours each day, it seems they would rather spend that time at work trying to make some extra money for their kids' college fund. Instead of spending forty dollars on a hair stylist, they would rather spend it on their children's orthodontist. Face it, dads tend let themselves go. Where are their priorities?

And I wonder: where would most dads wear a fancy $350 shirt? A soccer game? A school play? A Chuck E.

Cheese birthday party? Walking the dog their kids promised to take care of? The other dads would laugh at him. The moms would think he's getting a divorce or having an affair.

Dads and fashion don't mix. A lot of dads forget to ask themselves some basic fashion questions before leaving the house. Does the black neoprene knee brace go with the plaid shorts? What's the right color of old dirty, disgusting sweatpants to wear to the supermarket? Are the young kids still wearing suspenders? Will that rabbit-skin hat with the big earflaps be warm enough?

Despite the advertising, even the department stores know that dads are a lost cause. Walk into any department store and you will find eight floors of women's clothing and one-eighth of a floor of men's clothing. These people know that the Y chromosome contains a defective shopping gene. If they depended on male shoppers to make a living, they'd be out of business. If it doesn't involve beer, cars, or sports, why buy it?

It doesn't help that the older men get, the cheaper they get. They can't believe how much more things cost now than when they were kids. If I ever want to push my

Dad's buttons, all I have to do is tell him how much I spent on a new car or how much I owe on my credit cards, or how much I spend renting an apartment. Then he will tell me, for the thousandth time, that he bought his first house for what I was paying a year in rent, and that being in debt was like stealing from yourself. If I really want to drive him crazy, all I have to say is, "You know, for only six bucks, it's not a bad cup of coffee."

"Six dollars! For a cup of coffee!" And he will tell me, once again, how his father had to work six long days on the back of a horse to make six dollars. Everyone in my family can tell you exactly what the price of a gallon of milk and the price of a dozen eggs was in 1933. We all know what his first job paid in 1937 and how much it cost for a gallon of gas. He'd never hire anyone to do something he could do just as well. Until they became metric and computerized, he'd do all the car repairs himself. "Hire a roofer to put on a new roof? When I can do it myself?" "Hire a painter to paint the house? When I can paint it myself?" "Hire an electrician to rewire the house? When I can do it myself?" If he ever spent money on a plumber or a carpenter or a mason, I never heard about it.

He saved a lot, but the roof always leaked, the paint always peeled, and we learned to wear rubber-soled shoes when we turned on the lights.

The $350 shirt is not going to work for Dad, so let's see what else they're pushing for Father's Day. Oh, here's an ad for a watch. A nice $6,000 watch. But can I afford the stroke he would have when he learns the price?

Riding the Mechanic's Bull

My "Check Engine" light is on again. So I unlatched the hood and took a look. Sure enough, it was still there. It looked good, too. Right where it's supposed to be. In the middle. Lots of hoses and wires and belts all over the place. They were a little dirty, but hey, I live on a dirty street. You have to expect a little dirt might get under the hood. That was enough checking for me. I slammed down the hood but still, the light wouldn't go out. Where's the "OK, I checked it" button?

Of course, there is no such thing; that would be too easy. I've fallen into the "Check Engine" scam and there's no escaping it.

"What could cause the 'Check Engine' light to go on?" I asked Roger, my mechanic.

"Oh, lots of things—my Junior starting college, Betsy buying new living room furniture, that vacation we want to take to Orlando, my daughter deciding to marry that bonehead she's been seeing—it all depends. You'd have to bring it in."

"Is it OK for me to keep driving it?"

"Sure, I don't need the money that fast."

"I meant would it be *safe* for me to drive it or do I need to have you look at it right away?"

"I never thought of it that way. Let me think. I'm sure it's safe. What's the worst that could possibly happen? Your car suddenly stops dead on the Interstate while an eighteen-wheeler full of steel girders going sixty-five is tailgating you? Don't be such a worry wart, you wouldn't even feel it. By the way, have you filled out that donor card on the back of your license? Not that there'd be many good parts left, but what's left of your skin could still be used to help many, many people. Don't be selfish."

"Thanks for the concern, but what could make the light go on?"

"A thousand things, from something as simple as a loose gas cap to a leaky head gasket. I'm guessing leaky head gasket because we just bought a condo in Boca, but I hate to get into the hypothetical. It could mean so many things: it could mean that your car is no longer under warranty, it could mean you're late for an oil change, it could mean that you should bring it back to the dealer so he can show you all the new stuff in his showroom that will make that piece of junk you're driving now look like a Third World jitney, it could mean that the 'Check Engine' light needs to be replaced."

"So you're saying it's just a big scam."

"Not at all. It's probably that catalytic thingamajig that reduces emissions. I'm pretty sure you can't pass inspection if that's not working."

"But you're the inspector."

"Yeah, it's funny how that works. It's almost like I could make up anything I wanted to make that light go off."

"There's no way I can check it myself?"

"Please. This takes sophisticated equipment and years of training."

"A kid at the auto parts store told me he could do it for twenty bucks."

"Did I say years of training? I meant fifteen minutes. But he can't fix it."

"Roger, I'm trying to figure out how much this is going to cost me."

"What can I tell you? It could run anywhere from a day at the spa for Betsy to a new ATV for our summer place. Somewhere in that range. But don't worry, I won't do any work unless you approve it."

"Maybe it'd be cheaper to buy a new car than to keep throwing money at this one. Eight hundred here, six hundred there, it's starting to add up. Haven't you replaced everything on this car at least once?"

"You've still got the original back seat. And the ashtray and cup holders work fine. Are you sure you want to take such a drastic step? Keep it another year. Junior's been begging me for that Guitar Hero game."

Waiting for Dr. Godot

It's nice that Dr. Godot has a whole room just for waiting. It's so convenient. But it makes you wonder. If he called it the "Wasting Your Valuable Time Room" would his patients sit there so willingly? Calling it a waiting room makes it sound as if waiting is the most normal thing in the world that we could be doing with our time. We're not fuming, we're not steaming, we're not twiddling our thumbs because it's a waiting room—not a fuming room, not a steaming room, not a twiddling-our-thumbs room.

There must be some really thoughtless doctors out there who take patients as soon as they show up at their scheduled time and don't give them any time to wait. But as soon as they are found, they are drummed out of the profession. Of course, it's not just doctors that make us wait. Airports are composed almost entirely of waiting rooms. They have acres and acres of waiting rooms. The waiting rooms are so humongous they have book stores and restaurants and souvenir stands and coffee bars in them. If the airlines really thought every flight would leave on time do you think they'd build such gigantic waiting rooms? Maybe the ticket price for air travel should drop each hour you have to wait. Wait one hour, ten dollars off the ticket price, two hours, you save twenty dollars and so on. For every hour you sit in the plane on the tarmac, fifty dollars off the ticket price. Under this system, most of us could make money by flying.

My appointment with Dr. Godot was for two o'clock; I still haven't seen him and it's now three o'clock. But if I had shown up at three o'clock I would have missed my appointment. *I* would have been late. That seems so one-sided. If I have an appointment with Dr.Godot, why doesn't Dr.Godot have an appointment with me? Oh sure, I understand that there are emergencies. I watch those hospital shows on TV. Well, I used to, but not anymore. It's too unreal.

On TV, entire families walk right into the Emergency Room without waiting; Mom, Dad, five or six children all wailing and screaming, "Don't let her die!" She has a bad case of psoriasis. The psoriasis family never fills out a form; they never wait a minute. The doctors on television all look like fashion models. Dr. Godot looks like Jack Klugman.

On television no one ever waits. A show called *WR* wouldn't stand a chance. Who would want to watch a big room full of people moaning and sneezing and bleeding from the forehead and NOT being treated?

At least Dr. Godot tries to class up his waiting room and make it comfortable. He hangs pieces of fine art, and the chairs are big and soft. I even know what he does in his spare time thanks to the magazines scattered around. Godot subscribes to *High Class Ski Resorts*, *Exclusive Golfing in Europe*, *Expensive Antiques Monthly*, *Cigar and Wine Bore* and *Cayman Islands Tax Shelters*.

There is a very fine reproduction of a large, ancient Etruscan vase in his waiting room placed between two chairs. It's waist-high. The classy effect is spoiled, however, by the hand-printed note taped above the vase that says, "This is not a garbage can!"

How can they be so sure? Maybe that's exactly what the Etruscans used it for. Garbage pick-up on the ides and nones of every month. The Etruscans are probably having a good laugh that Godot paid six grand for it at auction.

Finally at three-thirty the nurse told me the doctor would see me now.

"I'm so sorry about the delay," said Dr. Godot, "but there was an emergency. A man collapsed out at the golf course."

"Is he all right?"

"I suppose so; EMS took care of him. But it held up our foursome for an hour."

It's a Fun Job, But Someone's Got to Do It

D riving past a fast food restaurant today I spotted a sign out in front that said, "FUN JOBS! Apply Inside." Fun jobs. The sign seemed to contradict something my Dad used to say to me at least five or six times a week when I was a teenager: "If it was fun, they wouldn't call it work." His other favorite sayings were "That bed won't make itself," "That lawn won't mow itself," "This house won't paint itself," and the one we always hated to hear, "That finger won't sew itself back on."

Still I wonder, what could these fun fast-food jobs possibly be? Cleaning the restrooms? It's not that much fun. If it was fun, kids would do it at home. If it was fun, the customers would pick up after themselves. Perhaps that's why so many places have stopped cleaning their restrooms—it's just not fun, it's like, a job.

That would also explain why there are no paper towels in the paper towel dispenser, why the place smells of antiseptic spray instead of soap and elbow grease, and why there is some kind of nasty mold growing under the sink. Cleaning: it's just not fun.

Microwaving the food sounds like fun. But after the first four or five hours, I'll bet teenagers figure out it's not as much fun as playing "Grand Theft Auto" while locked in their bedrooms. Cooking food all day long is not as much fun as playing video games all day long and then ordering in pizza when you get hungry. If only they would pay us to play video games. That would be a fun job!

There's not really much of anything in a fast-food restaurant that would qualify as a fun job once you've done it a few hundred thousand times. Emptying huge bins of trash all day long, mopping floors, policing the parking lot—not fun, not fun, not fun.

A fun job would be, say, testing suntan lotion. Fifty thousand a year to start, no experience necessary. That's the kind of place that should have a sign outside that says, "FUN JOBS! Apply Inside."

Being a hotel-fortune heiress is probably a fun job. No wasting time getting a college degree; no bothering with inconvenient job interviews. Just buy a closet full of ten-thousand-dollar dresses and start going to nightclubs. The great part is you pick your own hours and you're your own boss. Now that's fun. The bad news? No paid vacations.

Movie stars look like they have lots of fun on the job. The sign out in front of most Hollywood studios should say, "FUN JOBS! Apply Inside." No one asks actors to clean the studio parking lot, someone's always fussing with their hair and makeup, they get driven to work in a limousine and they get an RV for a dressing room. Best of all, the minimum wage for movie stars is a few million dollars a year. And there's a good opportunity for advancement.

Here's the perfect first fun job for a young high school student: Cell Phone Tester. The kids would work on commission. The phone companies would give them a cut of their parent's bill, say fifteen percent. So on a hundred-dollar phone bill, your high-schooler would only make fifteen dollars, but if they can drive your bill up to five or six hundred dollars, they could make as much or more than any part-time, not-so-fun job would pay them.

Some of them might even be able to test two phones at a time. They wouldn't have to learn how to make change the way they would at that fun fast-food restaurant job, and they wouldn't have to wear a uniform or a hairnet or a name tag. It'd be like hardly working at all. What a fun job!

A Learner's Permit to Kill

Remember when James Bond out-golfed Goldfinger by one stroke? Bond never practiced, but he played golf like a pro. I play golf three or four times a week and I get worse, not better.

Bond walks through Q's laboratory, picks up the latest gadget and knows how it works instantly—without ever having read the manual. I can't even do something new on my cell phone—*with* the instructions in front of me—for a week.

It takes me fifteen minutes in a rental car to figure out how to turn on the lights and the radio, and to learn how to adjust the seats. James Bond jumps into the world's newest and most sophisticated fighter jet and, never having seen it before, he flies it like he's a Blue Angel.

I go to a casino and I lose every single hand, every roll of the dice. Bond? It's like the place is his personal cash machine. He knows all the dealers and all the bartenders. He's just come to withdraw a few hundred thousand dollars.

The computer I've been using for years still figures out new and exciting ways to frustrate me. Bond walks into a strange office and downloads secret files onto a hard disk disguised as a mole on his cheek with the aid of a paper clip and a fountain pen. Could he please come to my house and get my printer and my computer to talk to one another?

Bond flies from London to Rio and before he gets to his hotel, he has three dirt bike chases, one parachute jump, and pilots a mini-submarine to a yacht in the harbor, where he finally meets the second-most-attractive woman on Earth and goes to bed with her.

That evening Bond, who carried no luggage, will turn up at a casino in a custom-made tuxedo that can be turned inside-out to become a Level 5 Haz-Mat self-contained breathing suit. The great mystery of all James Bond films is not how Bond is going to stop the villain from destroying the planet, but how James Bond's clothes got to his hotel room. You never see him carry any luggage. You never see him standing at the baggage carousel. Who wouldn't golf, who wouldn't ski, who wouldn't program their own computer, who wouldn't travel if it were really this easy?

I flew from New York to London last year and I have never been so exhausted in my life. The people in First Class looked tired; the people in Business Class looked tired; the people in my class, Abusive Coach looked clubbed and beaten. The flight was so numbing it only took one flight attendant to tie down our drunken air-rage passenger. Nobody on the plane was up for *one* dirt bike chase, much less three of them.

My feet hurt, my clothes were rumpled. Don't 007's feet ever hurt? Doesn't he ever get jet lag? Does Bond ever spend two hours going through customs? I wasn't met at the airport by a sexy female driver with a double-entendre name like Vi Agra who would flirt with me as she drove me to my swank hotel in her brand new BMW convertible.

No, I took mass transit to what had once been a meager one-star hotel, but was now seedy and faded. My hotel room had no grand staircase, no gilt furniture, no fresh-cut flowers, no wet bar, no spectacular view. On the plus side, there was no one in the room waiting to kill me. How could there be? There wouldn't have been enough room for the two of us in such a tiny, cramped room. But I did feel very James Bondish. Thanks to the airline, I, too, was now luggage-free.

Hair Today,
Gone Tomorrow

"Did you just wake up?" asked Ralph the counterman as he poured out my breakfast coffee. "No."

"Something looks different. Did you put on a ton of weight?"

"No, thank you, it's just a new haircut."

"You paid for that?"

"Yes, I did. And unlike you, I had to pay full price for having so much hair. You must get, oh what, a seventy-five percent discount?"

I shouldn't have said that. For the next two weeks I will get runny eggs and day-old coffee. Ralph's service will be slower than usual, there will be no refills, and it'll take forever to get the check. But Ralph knows I've been trying to find a new barber ever since Charlie went to Florida two years ago after he developed carpal tunnel syndrome.

"From the repetitive motion of giving everyone the exact same haircut for thirty years," Sue contributed.

"He didn't give everyone the same haircut. He was an artist."

"Yeah. So was the guy who painted the dogs sitting around the table playing poker."

Since Charlie's been gone I've been to every place in town and no one seems to get my hair right, or care.

Toné's House of Hair (formerly Tony's Barber Shop) in the mall won't take reservations. Each time I go, someone new cuts my hair. Someone who wasn't there last time.

"What happened to Jeannie?" I asked Madame Toné, the proprietor.

"She's having a baby."

"I was here two weeks ago. She didn't mention it. She didn't even look pregnant."

"Did I say having a baby? I meant she's in a safe house hiding from her boyfriend. But Tiffany's free."

Tiffany has rainbow-colored hair—blue, red, yellow, and purple, with black tips. Yeah, I know, black isn't in the rainbow, but then, neither is hair. Her eyebrow, nose, lower lip and ears are pierced. She is wearing all black and zippers. I'm guessing she's about forty years younger than I am.

"How do you like it?" she asked, running a hand through my grey hair.

"Oh, as Goth as you can make it." She laughed and did a great job. She gave me a haircut that didn't look like I'd just gotten a haircut. Finally, I thought, someone who understands me, someone who knows that I don't want to look like a person who spends a lot of time fussing with his hair but I don't want to look like Rasputin on a bad hair day, either. Tiffany and I bonded; from now on, she would be the only person to touch my hair. Two weeks later she was gone.

"Don't tell me she's hiding from a boyfriend," I told Madame Toné.

"No, she was having money problems."

"Really? She looked so busy. I'm sure she got good tips, too."

"Yes, that was her money problem. Someone offered her more money to leave here."

"Where'd she go?"

Toné looked at me as if I had just crawled out of a Paris sewer. "David's free," she said. She pronounced it "Da Veed."

David had a buzz cut that looked like he had a five o'clock shadow where his hair should have been except for one long lock right in the middle of his forehead pasted into a spit curl. David was wearing huge hoop earrings. My haircut that day was not successful. It looked very much as if someone had just cut my hair—with an axe.

"You'll be able to get into all the clubs now," he said.

Next I went to Nick's, the jock barbershop with all the sports magazines and pictures of sports heroes covering the walls and featuring Nick's personal collection of autographed footballs, baseballs, basketballs, golf balls, and hockey pucks. Nick wanted to carve the logo of his favorite team into my hair. I said if I'm going to be their billboard, they should pay me. Talk to my agent. After that, Nick lost interest.

There's a bald guy at the other end of the counter getting another refill of hot, fresh coffee while mine sits, cold and half-empty. I don't need a new barber, I need a new hangout.

The First Thanksgiving Family Feud

Historians all agree—the Pilgrim's First Thanksgiving was a one-time event. It wasn't turned into a yearly celebration until Abraham Lincoln made it official during the middle of the Civil War, almost 250 years later. A newly-discovered cache of papers composed by the original passengers of the Mayflower may explain why.

"Never again," writes John Alden. "Six long hours we have spent looking at the hind end of a horse on the overly crowded road to the house of my parents and lo, for what? To see my brother with whom I barely speak and his harpy wyfe who so disrespecteth me and mine in a backhanded way? He starteth acting like a wee childe from the time we stepped from the carriage until the time we departed. He bringeth up small jealousies and grievances from our youth long ago. His unhappiness is like a contagion, a pustule that never heals. 'Letteth it go and getteth a life,' he has made me wish to scream, and more times than one.

"One unpleasantry follows another as I suffer my uncles and aunts to runneth on and on about my cousins—how well they are doing, how much money they are sending to their parents, what comely grandchildren they have produced. Yet I knoweth these same cousins. They would soil themselves if they were ever made to do a day's work.

"They wish their parents dead and spend their days making plans to squander their inheritance in a warmer clime. Their small children hear not the word 'no' and understandeth not its meaning. They runneth around and screameth all day when peace and quiet is called for.

"And my wyfe cares not for the way my mother prepareth the meal. 'She useth not oysters in the fowl's stuffing,' she rails at me. 'She putteth not the bird in a paper bag in the hearth.' It maketh me fatigued to hear such words. Yet Priscilla's own stuffing would not winneth any prize, even in the land of my birth where they can taste not the difference between soup and soap. She knoweth not, but secretly I giveth my portions of her bounty to the hound beneath the table. It teacheth him not to beg.

"My wyfe speaks ill of none, yet I can tell from the bearing of her body that she would rather be ducking witches on a cold day in December than in the company of my family and their offspring. As if her family be a barrel of salted fish. Her sisters make it well known that their spouses buy them more kitchen tools than I, and that the corn from their labor is bigger and better than that of my own. They maketh my head hurt. Were they not aboard, the journey of the Mayflower could have been as a fun ship. With them, it was as the hate boat.

"It occurred to me suddenly that we may have left the wood stove on at home. Priscilla volunteered that it may be true as she had often noticed my forgetful habits. Happily, we fled the festivities. On the road home we sat in silence for many hours. 'Let us hope we can do this again next year,' at last I spoke. It got a hearty laugh as Priscilla knew I was in perfect jest. In truth, you could not make us do that again were two hundred and fifty years to pass. And for that we gave thanks."

Ask Little Miss Know-it-all

Dear Little Miss Know-It-All,

My fiancé and I want to hold our wedding in an historic, eighty-room castle in France and fly all our friends and family in for free. At the reception we want a twelve-course French meal served by waiters wearing outfits of my own design. The guests must wear all black or all white. I've already told my friends they can't be bridesmaids unless they weigh under a hundred and two pounds.

The bad news is that my Dad says he won't pay for it. He thinks we're too young (sheesh, I'll be twenty in three years). He said he'd pay for a wedding in our local church if we invite the same old boring friends and family we see every day. And only if my fiancé, Tommy, gets a job. What should I do?

—Why Me in Massachusetts

Dear Why Me,

Can't you see that your control freak Dad is trying to wreck your life? You've got to get out of that house as soon as possible by marrying Tommy. He sounds dreamy. As soon as you're married, you'll find that all your problems will magically disappear. Suddenly you'll be happy with the way you look and you'll be comfortable with your weight. Everyone will suddenly like you, even those snobby kids at your old high school. I think you should pay for the wedding yourself by maxing out all your credit cards, yours and Tommy's. Besides, after the wedding you won't need any money, because you'll have each other. Maybe your stupid father doesn't know it, but it's a well-known fact that the more money you spend on your wedding, the better your marriage will be. Don't let anyone, especially your unbelievably stupid father, step on your dreams. I wouldn't even invite him to the wedding.

Dear Little Miss Know-It-All,

I'm sixteen and I want to be a football star or a basketball star. Or maybe a golf legend. The problem is that my parents want me to apply to one of those colleges that barely even has a sports team, like Harvard or M.I.T. just because I get good grades. They want me to be a scientist or a professor. How do I convince them that being smart is a dumb career move?

—Concerned in Mineola

Dear Concerned,

Sometimes you wonder where parents get these silly ideas. A scientist. As if Nike is ever going to pay you millions of dollars to wear a swoosh logo on your lab coat.

Still, let's get real. You may never become a thirty-million-dollar-a-year athlete. You may only be a five- or six-million-dollar-a-year athlete. If you don't think you can live with that kind of bitter disappointment, you might as well go to Harvard. I suppose it can't hurt.

Dear Little Miss Know-It-All,

I plan to win *American Idol* this year, but I'm worried about what to do with the million dollars after I win.

You're the only person I can talk to. Should I spend it on fancy cars, designer clothes and jewelry or should I just waste it on silly stuff? What do you think?

—Tired of Waiting

Dear Tired,

Spend it all, baby! And why wait until you win? Spend it now and pay it back after you win.

Dear Little Miss Know-It-All,

I met a guy on a computer dating service and he says he'd like to see me in person but he can't afford to travel all the way. He lives two states away and he's really cute. Should I send him the six hundred dollars he needs to get here and back, or not?

—Confused in Columbus

Dear Confused,

Is six hundred enough? He may think you're cheap. Why not send him a thousand to show him what a nice person you are? He sounds like a nice guy, I'm sure he'll pay you back. After all, you met him on a computer. What could go wrong? You know, it's funny that he can afford a computer but not airfare. I don't know what that's all about, but I'm sure it will all become clear once you meet him.

The Storm of the Century

"Snow! There is a five percent chance of snow tomorrow!" There is a look of panic on the weatherman's face. It's as if he were announcing that car-sized balls of flaming magnesium mixed with nuclear waste were going to be falling out of the sky tomorrow. Snow! All plant and animal life will cease to exist. *Dancing with the Stars* may be postponed. And traffic will be a nightmare! Oh, the humanity!

"Snow! Sure, it's the middle of winter in North America but who could have predicted a disaster like this? Snow! One to two inches expected! More in higher elevations! Some drifting may occur! Run for your lives!" Biff the weatherman is shaking. He forgot to kiss his wife and kids goodbye this morning and now this—two inches of snow expected! Will they ever see each other again?

Where Biff leaves off, the other reporters begin.

"Snow! What could be worse, Biff? A giant asteroid slamming into the Earth at 17,000 miles a second? A black hole swallowing the entire planet? Swearing live at the Grammy Awards? Why weren't we warned about this months ago? Who's to blame? The mayor? The governor? NASA? Stay tuned; Michelle and I will be interviewing the chief meteorologist of the National Weather Service to get the details on this totally unexpected disaster.

"Snow! Count your children! Fill a tub with fresh water! Run to a nearby grocery store and buy every single thing you can. Strip it clean; you never know when you'll be able to get out of the house again. It may be hours, but then it may be *several* hours. Be prepared.

"Snow experts are advising people to stand away from their windows and shut the curtains. Watch the snow on TV and avoid the risk of snow blindness. We'll be running a special report on snow blindness tonight right after *Celebrity Wart Removals*.

"And what about the possibility of avalanches? Dr. Maxwell D. Pushface of the National Center of Avalanche Spokespeople assures us that they rarely happen in flat parts of the country like ours, but that doesn't mean we're in the clear. There's always a first time.

"One tragic death has already been attributed to the coming snowstorm. One-hundred-and-fourteen-year-old Maude Fitzwilly was found dead in her living room on Elm Street earlier today, sitting in front of a television. Emergency service workers at the scene said snow panic syndrome may have contributed to her untimely demise. Bob and Michelle will be discussing snow panic syndrome, or SPS as it is known, with Dr. Carter T. Cuffman later in the show.

"And in a second snow-related incident, Byron Zmults of Hendersonville plowed his '83 Dodge into a bridge abutment on Alabaster Road. Police say he was on his way to buy a few more cases of beer and some more marijuana so he wouldn't have to leave his house during tomorrow's storm. His blood-alcohol level was three times the legal limit, but Zmults said he never would have been driving on a suspended license if it hadn't been a snow-related emergency.

"Later tonight, right after *When Cousins Marry*, we'll be talking to Dr. D. Byron Latchkey, who says there are things called 'coats' and 'hats' that can actually be worn outside during a snowstorm. With all we know about snow nowadays, it's hard to believe, but he says that once people used to go out in the snow and play in it and enjoy it.

"But that was back in the simple days before modern newscasting. We didn't know then what we know now about killer snow. Did you know, for example, that no two flakes are alike? If that doesn't say 'Danger' I don't know what does. Actually, the government is now spending billions on a program to clone snowflakes so for the first time in history, we can have two snowflakes that are exactly alike, which may lead to 'stackable snow,' but right now that is just a theory.

"Stay tuned to our non-stop coverage of 'The Killer Storm of the Millennium' and you may be one of the lucky few to make it out alive."

One Man's Trash Is Another Man's Garbage

"Do you have any idea what this ten-dollar bill is worth?"

"I have no idea. We never had it appraised. My dad gave it to me, like, a year ago. But it says 1973 on it so it must be worth something. That's why we brought it to *Antiques Sideshow*."

"Well, I have some good news and some bad news for you. The good news is, that at a well-advertised auction, it would bring ten dollars. Does that shock you?"

"Totally. Unbelievable! It's amazing to think that something that old could be worth anything. My wife was going to throw it out but I said, 'Whoa, that might still be worth two or three bucks.'"

"Now the bad news—it's only worth 6.25 Euros. Or to put it another way, if you had bought ten Euros with this in 2002, it would now be worth $16. Does *that* surprise you?"

"Well, I guess it does. What is a Yuro? Some kind of car?"

"Thank you for coming. Now let's go to Skip and Chad, the Furniture Twins, to see what they've discovered."

"We're here with Mavis Bucktooth and a Colonial highboy she's brought in. Do you know anything about this piece, Mavis?"

"Not much. I think my grandmother bought it from some antique mall or something when they went out of business. All I know is that she wouldn't let any of us kids play with it or kick it or put our cigarettes out on it. What a control freak. When she died, my brothers got all the good stuff, the liquor and the TV tables. All I got was this old piece of junk."

"Let's take a look at it. Skip, this secondary wood on the bottom of the drawers tells me that this was made in Boston, on Blueblood Street, I'm guessing here, but I would say in the 300 block."

"I couldn't agree more, Chad. As you can see from this delicate carving, it was made in either August or September 1763, probably on a Tuesday."

"I couldn't agree more, Skip. It does have some condition issues, though. Were you the one who painted it, Mavis? You did? Painting it high-gloss pink and adding sequins has lessened the value quite a bit. In its original condition, if it had all its original hardware, it would have been worth $120,000. As you have chainsawed the legs off and replaced the original pulls with red Lego pieces, I would say, for insurance purposes, this is worth—are you ready? Minus forty dollars. Because if you leave it here, that's what we'll have to charge you to take it to the dump. Does that surprise you?"

"No, I knew Grandma wouldn't leave me anything that was worth anything. She was a crazy old lady; her house was full of junk like this. We chopped it up and burned most of it."

"Your host Charles St. John here. Could someone please revive the Furniture Twins and get them off the floor? Now we'll hop to the Experts' Table for some more quick appraisals."

"Thank you, Charles. What we have here is a Ming Dynasty vase, certainly made for the Chinese royal family. I would say its value is somewhere in the 12 to 14 thousand dollar range."

"Oh, thank you, that's great. I can't wait to tell . . . Ahhhhhh!"

"I was just about to tell him not to trip over Chad's body. I don't think that can be put back together. Maybe he can use the pieces to make a nice mosaic table for the patio, estimated value, eighty dollars."

"This is a very nice Georgian silver service. Do you know its provenance?"

"Its what?"

"Its provenance, its story, its history. Where did it come from?"

"Oh, yeah, its provenance. It, ah, fell off a truck and Joey Stink Eye give it to me to pay off a loan."

"I'd have it insured for . . ."

"Insured? I'm, how do you say, self-insured. How much would a fen . . . a third party give me for it, no questions asked?"

"Four thousand."

"Joey, if you're watching this, you still owe me two grand!"

Psssst! Don't Tell Anyone!
It's the Secret

Shhhh! Promise not to tell anyone, it's a secret! I heard about it on Oprah Winfrey's show, so practically nobody knows about it, but I'm passing it along to you because, well, I'm one of those people who just can't keep a secret.

When my old neighbor Bob told me he was having an affair with the school lunch lady, I only told five or six people, tops, and before you know it, it was all over town. Who could have guessed? Bob now lives in a cardboard box down on Main Street; his wife moved to San Diego.

When I told the congregation that I ran into Mrs. Townsend at the liquor store, I had no idea that her ex-husband would use it as an excuse to try to take away her kids. Funny thing, it turns out she wasn't buying liquor, she was asking the owner to donate money to the Community Chest. The good news? She's almost paid off all the lawyer's fees.

Pete and Andre haven't spoken to me since I introduced them as "my good gay friends" at the Rotary. Sorry, guys, I thought *everyone* knew.

In short, if you want to keep a secret, don't mention it to me. Which is why I was so surprised to hear Oprah talking so openly about *The Secret*. If she keeps talking about it, it'll be on all the morning shows, it'll be on the national news, it'll be on the Internet, it might sell two million copies of the book. Then it's not a secret! So shssssh!

The Secret says you can get anything you want just by thinking positive thoughts about it. You want a million dollars? All you have to do is think positively that you need a million dollars and *poof!* You'll get it. You want to lose weight? You want to find Mr. Right? You want a better job? You think positively about it, and you'll get it. That's the secret of *The Secret*.

Oh, there's a lot of New Age, mumbo-jumbo, EST, "we are stardust, we are golden," happy-hippy talk that goes along with it—energy is thought and since the entire Universe is made of energy by thinking thoughts you can just tap into the power of the cosmos and . . . oh, who cares as long as it works? Right now I'm thinking how positive it would be to have one million dollars in the bank instead of the eleven dollars that was in there yesterday. I'm not thinking about all the taxes I'd have to pay on a million dollars; I'm not thinking about how many begging relatives would start knocking on my door once I have it.

I wonder if I should tell Bob about *The Secret*? I don't think he gets TV in his box and I still feel bad about the whole lunch lady thing. He should think positive thoughts about getting his old life back. Or at least he could think about getting a new box. The one he has now is pretty rank.

Memo to self: Stop by the bank this afternoon and see if that million's been added to my account yet.

Some people might ask, "Exactly what's the difference between 'wishing' and 'daydreaming' and *The Secret*?" I would answer them by saying, "You are bringing me down, man. You're full of negative thoughts and I hope you die in a fiery car crash. But in a positive way. You don't think they'd let Oprah put this on TV if it was just a bunch of hooey, do you?"

When I think of all the years I've wasted thinking that my lack of education and my police record were holding me back, I could just spit. Whoops! A negative thought. It's that kind of thinking that will lose me my million dollars. Whoops! That was another negative thought.

The bank just called. I'm overdrawn, again! By three dollars. Because my copy of *The Secret* cost thirteen dollars plus tax. That's when total and complete enlightenment hit me. It's not knowing "the secret" that makes anyone a millionaire, it's writing things like *The Secret* that makes them millionaires. By the way, have you heard about *the key*? No? It can unlock your potential and change your life. Look for my new book *The Key* coming to a bookstore near you, soon. Don't keep it a secret.

Naked Breakfast, Lunch, and Dinner

I saw the first sign of summer today: a bare-chested, overweight man on a riding mower. We averted our eyes and kept driving and just when we thought we were safe, we saw another one. You don't see this much skin in a Calvin Klein ad. I wanted to roll down the car window and yell "For God's sake, man, think of the children!" but Sue locks the windows when I'm in the car with her. According to her, yelling out the car window at strangers is "antisocial behavior."

Antisocial? I'm trying to help the poor guy. Maybe if he put on a shirt and bought a push mower he'd drop a few pounds and have six-pack abs by the end of the summer. It's one thing for Matthew McConaughey to run around half-naked, it's another for an Orson Welles impersonator. This is just a guess, but I would say the ratio of shirtless, well-proportioned men using riding mowers to big jelly-bellied men is roughly, oh, one to 99. Now, I don't have a perfect body and I'm not trying to promote silly, unhealthy, unattainable, perfect bodies. All I'm trying to promote is wearing a shirt while you mow the lawn. Is that too much to ask?

It is perfectly natural for men, especially older, bald men who don't eat right, don't exercise and don't wax their backs to have love handles and sagging pecs. That doesn't mean I want to see them while they mow the lawn. When did suburbia become a half-nudist camp? Did I miss the "we don't have to wear shirts anymore" memo? Was I out of town the day we voted to start doing yard work naked? And what is the point of having a beautiful lawn if you're going to spoil it by being on it? Let me put it this way: would you put a statue of yourself mowing the lawn with your shirt off on your front lawn? Unless the answer is yes, keep your shirt on.

Why is it that the people with the worst bodies wear the most revealing clothes? Every New Year's Day when the local Polar Bear Club goes for their annual dive in the ice-cold water it's always the biggest, most out-of-shape polar bear who is wearing the tiniest Speedo. At the ball game, the guys who take off their shirts and paint their bodies with team logos and slogans are never the guys with ripped, six-pack, washboard stomachs but the ones with the biggest, largest beer bellies. It looks as if a giant orange Jell-O mold has escaped and will soon start crushing innocent bystanders. Men with spindle legs insist on wearing shorts; women with Frisbee-sized bellybuttons are wearing midriff-baring fashion.

They all suffer from a disease that gets too little attention in the press—Reverse Anorexia. They think they are skinny and beautiful when they are not. They are like the *American Idol* contestants who think they can sing but cannot. Some may suffer from Amnesiac Bulimia—they binge but they forget to purge—but the results are the same.

Not that we need to starve ourselves like runway models, and God knows, I don't, but that is exactly why I wear lots of clothes, so you don't have to see how I've let myself go. And I am all for being comfortable. If you want to watch TV at home in your underwear looking like a Nick Nolte mug shot, be my guest. If you want to wear the most tattered and torn things you own while you are out in the back yard gardening, go to it. If you're planning to make a surprise appearance on *Cops*, being shirtless makes loads of fashion sense. But if you're taking the kids to Six Flags or Disney World in an air-conditioned minivan with backseat DVRs, you could wear some decent clothes.

There are some basic fashion rules. Unless your son is playing basketball in the van or is on his way to a basketball game, he shouldn't be wearing long, baggy, nasty, polyester basketball shorts. Unless your twelve-year-old daughter has a full-time job at Hooters or Victoria's Secret, she shouldn't be wearing crotch-high shorts and a Dale Evans vest with no shirt on underneath it. If you never exercise, stop pretending you do by wearing warm-up togs; you're not fooling anyone. Showing lots of skin is sexy if you've got the body of a *Sports Illustrated* swimsuit model; if not, not. That goes for men, too. Unless you're competing for a swimming medal in the Olympics, no one wants to see you in a Speedo. Absolutely no one. I'm not kidding, it's an offense against God and nature. You may be comfortable but you're making the rest of us sick.

Years ago we used to have a neighbor who would take off his shirt when he mowed the lawn, but he was a male model working on his tan. Women in the neighborhood would always find time to do yard work when he mowed. They would suddenly have an urge to trim the roses or train the vines or just sweep the walk that didn't really need sweeping. But few of the guys you see mowing their lawns shirtless are male models—unless they're the "after" models for nachos and beer.

It wasn't so long ago that you would see signs that said "No shirt, no shoes, no service." A few years later it turned into "No shirt, no shoes, no problem." How long before we start seeing "No shirt, no shoes, bride's side or groom's side?" or "No shirt, no shoes, how long did you know the deceased?" or "No shirt, no shoes, let's transplant this liver!"

If at First Class
You Don't Succeed . . .

Sometimes I wonder what is worse: the airlines or the passengers? On almost every flight I've taken the last few holidays, some couple will show up at the very last minute and have to be ushered on board with special airline handlers hustling them through the door, stowing their luggage for them, and getting them settled before rushing out so the crew can shut the cabin door, all under the hateful glare of all the other passengers who had the courtesy to show up an hour early.

Guess whose luggage will come off first? The late passengers'. So why should they bother to show up on time when they get rewarded for their bad behavior? They didn't have to wait in any lines. They didn't have to hang around the lounge for an hour sitting in chairs that have been specifically designed to be uncomfortable so homeless people won't want to live in them. They didn't have to hear "Would Mr. and Mrs. Liptfitter please report to the main ticket counter?" forty times over a nerve-shredding loudspeaker. They didn't have to hear it because, of course, they *are* the Liptfitters.

"Honey, this is so nice, it's nice to be late," said Mr. Liptfitter.

"Late? What do you know about being late?" she snapped. "If you had listened to me we would have been two minutes later and they would have given us seats in *First Class*. Don't talk to me about being late. I know how to be late."

The Lipfitters save in other ways by being late. Shops in the airport don't make any money on them. They depend on customers who must spend hours inside an airport with absolutely nothing to do but cruise the airport newsstands and bookstores. Who but the bored to death would buy magazines like *Funeral Home Management*, *Cubicle Cloth Designer*, *Pension Fund Skimmer*, *Meter Reader Monthly* and *Professional Llama Breeder*. What?

No *Amateur Llama Breeder*? What kind of a dump are you running here?

The bookstores are jammed with best-selling self-help books like *How to Pick a Self-Help Book, How to Get the Most Out of Self-Help Books, How to Get to the Front of This Store by Yourself,* and *Running a Billion Dollar Corporation Into the Dirt Made Simple.*

You can also pick up a six-dollar container of three individually-wrapped antacid tablets at any newsstand. Which you'll need, because the only thing you can buy to eat in the entire airport without having to stand in an hour-long line is a frozen yogurt and a bag of cashews. You'll never get into any of the good restaurants. Even if you do, you won't have time to eat there. Wait, isn't that the Liptfitters? They're sitting in the window of *L'Exquisite,* the fanciest restaurant in the entire airport. The line snakes from terminal A to terminal B and back again. How did they get in? They are laughing and drinking wine. She is eating medallions of beef with crabmeat garnish. He is having the *coq au vin.*

I can't worry about it now. I have accidentally dragged my coat through something wet and smelly on the men's room floor while trying to juggle my carry-on luggage and use the sink at the same time. On my way to the Baggage Claim, the youngish-looking Liptfitters glide past me on a beeping, chauffeur-driven electric cart normally used to ferry the elderly and infirm around airports. When I finally get to the car rental desk, my reserved car has already been rented because I had to wait an hour to find out I wasn't going to get my luggage and another hour to fill out the form. My car went to a nice, young couple—the Liptfitters.

"If you had only come here on time," said the clerk. "There's nothing we can do until morning."

Flight of the Bumblebee

These flat escalators at the airport are my favorite thing to play on. My sister Chrissy and me like to run in the wrong direction on them while big people try to get around us. It's like a Disney ride but you don't have to wait in line. But lots of times grown-ups don't even know it's a ride. Sometimes they don't even get on the escalators and walk in the boring old aisles even though they can see us having lots of fun on them. Other times they say things like, "This is not a playground, you could get hurt. Where are your parents?"

Clean your glasses, mister. They're standing right over there. Dad's reading the newspaper. Mom's on her cell phone. Hey, you want to run up the down escalator with me? Never mind, watch this. I can hang on this black, rubbery moving thing and then let it drag me along with it down the flat escalator. No, you can't do it, Chrissy. I just invented it and it's mine. Mom. Mom! MOM! MMMOMMM! Chrissy won't stop it!

I got brand new wheelie shoes. They're like sneakers and roller skates all in one. Watch this. Watch, Mom, watch! Mom. Mom! MOM! MMMOMMM! Too late. They never seem to be watching when I do the coolest stuff, like skate in and out of that line of people over there. It's like I'm invisible. Want to see me ram this shopping cart thingy into a window real hard? Watch!

Wow! Did you see that! The whole window shook. Did you see that old lady jump? Did you see everybody watching me? Except Mom and Dad. They miss all the good stuff. Mom! Mom, watch me! MOM! MMMOMMMM! Look!

Why do we have to see stupid, old grandma anyway? She doesn't let me touch anything in her stupid old house and it's just a bunch of stupid old stuff anyway. So what if her stupid old glass vase breaks. She acts like it's such a big deal. And who's Tiffany? None of her grand-kids are named Tiffany.

C'mon, let's play on the elevators. I can push all the buttons at once. Watch me hold the door open. See! It's trying to close but I put the shopping cart thing in it. Bang, bang, bang. Hey, don't do that, mister. I was playing with it first. Mom. Mom! MOM! MMMOMMM!

This is soooo boring. Mom. Mom! MOM! Get me another soda. I put this one down on the seat and it fell over. And I only took one sip. Let's sit somewhere else. This is all messy!

I don't WANT to play with Chrissy! NO, NO, NO, NO, NO! THIS *IS* MY INDOOR VOICE! MMMOMMM!

I don't have to go to the bathroom. I'm fine. I'm telling you, it's OK. I'm sure.

Chrissy, watch this. When I push this door open, it starts all those bells ringing. You try it. See? What'd I tell you? Have you ever heard anything that loud? Why is everybody running? Mom. Mom! MOM! MMMOMMM! My finger's stuck in the pay phone thingy! It hurts!

I don't care that we have to get on the plane right now. *I* have to go to the bathroom RIGHT NOW! Do you know what I mean?

Look at this, I can make all the sinks turn on at once. See that? Dad? Dad! DAD! DDDADDD!

What do you mean, they wouldn't hold the plane for us? They just left? Can we sue them? Can we? Like we sued that old school bus driver? You mean you settled for an upgrade to First Class on the next flight? OK. Just like last time, huh, Dad. Dad! DAD! DDDADDD!

When the Going Gets Tough, the Tough Go Shopping—for Guns

My brother-in-law Dave hunts pheasant and deer. A week before hunting season a gigantic new store for outdoorsmen opened and Dave took me along for a quick shopping trip. The store looks like one of those giant rustic log hotels you see in the national parks. It is made out of immense peeled logs, sixty or seventy feet long, as thick around as one of the oddly, prissily clean, brand-spanking-new pickup trucks in the parking lot. The building almost screams "Teddy Roosevelt Slept Here," except for the fact that it was obviously built yesterday. The testosterone is still wet.

Massive, twelve-point deer heads hang along either side of the main aisle, which leads to a forty-foot-tall man-made mountain in the center of the gigantic store. Climbing the mountain are stuffed trophy kills from raccoon to grizzly, from big-horned sheep to a giant sloth. It had one of everything that could be shot and stuffed except a Sasquatch.

"Why is it that being stuffed and mounted is good enough for a grizzly, but not good enough for, say, Grandpa?" I ask Dave. "I miss the old guy, but I've never visited his grave. Now I'm thinking, why did we spring for a stone, when for the price of a mid-range coffin we could have had him stuffed and put in the TV room? I think he'd go as well with our décor as any stuffed elk or mountain goat." Dave said nothing. He has learned not to listen to me.

Past Mount Mounted on the right is the Cold and Wet Department—an endless variety of canoes, kayaks, fishing rods, tackle, waders. On the left is hunter's paradise—rifles, shotguns, bows, arrows, deer stands. In between the two departments is everything the camper could desire—camp stoves, lightweight pots, flashlights, bug spray, tents, sleeping bags. Face it, if it's not in this store, it doesn't exist. An outdoor lover could drop a paycheck in here faster than you can say, "Hand me that brand-new snakebite kit."

I'm feeling a little uncomfortable in here. It is sooo manly. Even the underwear they sell has a camouflage pattern on it. I saw a guy walk by pushing two toddlers in a camouflage stroller. It's not like I'm Truman Capote, but I am an indoorsman. To me, game is something you play, not something you shoot. The only thing I have ever stalked is a dust bunny. And it got away. This is so far past my macho comfort level it's off the charts.

As we're walking around, I spot a rack of fleece jackets with a nylon shell on the outside for nineteen dollars apiece. I wear those synthetic fleece things around the house all the time because, unlike sweaters, they have pockets and you don't have to take them to the dry cleaners, you can just toss them in the wash.

Nineteen dollars? These things are a deal. So I take off my jacket and slip one off the hanger. Just as I stick my arm into the sleeve, a salesman rushes up and says in a megaphone-like voice, "Sir, those are women's jackets!"

The moment he speaks there is one of those strange moments when everything for half a second goes deadly quiet. You can hear him from the front of the store to the back.

I guess I should have known from the camouflage pantyhose that I was in the Women's Department, but I honestly didn't see them. They blended in too well with the camouflage bras and camouflage thongs.

To the store's credit, they didn't ask me to leave. It was Dave who suggested I might be more comfortable waiting for him in his truck.

It's My Lucky Day

The state lottery jackpot this week was one hundred and fifty-five million dollars. The line to buy tickets at the Gas 'n' Go Away snaked out the door and into the parking lot. Last week the prize was "only" eight million dollars. There was no line to buy tickets then. You could have walked right in and bought as many tickets as you wanted. But it seems gas station gamblers don't have much use for eight million dollars; however, they think that a hundred and fifty-five million might come in handy.

"Eight million? Chump change," says the guy in line in front of me. "If you think I'm going to stand in line for a lousy eight million dollars you got another think coming. You couldn't even quit your job with that kind of money. When you split it up between me, the wife, and the seven kids—why, it hardly comes to anything. If I was the kind of person who could be happy living on next to nothing, what the hell, I'd get a job."

Me, I was there just trying to buy a half-gallon of one-percent milk. There are only a hundred or so people in front of me, and the line is moving pretty quickly. Talk about luck; I'll be able to get out of here in half an hour or so. Meanwhile my line partner fills me (and everyone near us) in on the finer points of lottery betting.

"Now, I'm taking a big risk buying $200 worth of the hundred and fifty-five million tickets. What if I have to split it with someone? That would make me crazy. When I think of the time I've spent coming up with these numbers, and then to share the prize with somebody who just reached up and pulled the numbers out of thin air—I don't think I could handle it. To have to split the pot with an amateur? That would practically kill me. And then there's the taxes. That's the government for you. Always sticking their hand in your back pocket. They want to take half my money. It ain't fair. Who did all the work? I did! So between the taxes and the bum I have to share the prize with I'm down to thirty-nine million.

"Thirty-nine million. Is that supposed to make up for all those years I did without? Well, I didn't do without so much, but the wife and kids sure have. I'd hate to think they went without shoes and food for all those years for nothing."

My milk is room temperature. It's turned into some kind of gooey liquid cheese. I would go back and get more but the line has gotten longer. Besides, it's one-percent milk, who's going to know the difference?

Since I have been standing here the jackpot has gone up to a hundred and seventy million dollars. What happened to the fast, friendly service that the Gas 'n' Go Away is known for? You used to be able to come here buy some overpriced gas and some overpriced milk and get shoved right out. This is taking forever. My line mates are starting to quarrel over the best way to spend their winnings.

"Then, do I take it as a lump sum or spread it out over twenty years? Sure, the lump sum is a lot less cash, but then I can invest it myself instead of the state."

"What do you know about investing?" the guy behind us sneers. "If you know so much about the stock market why are you in line with the rest of us? Take the yearly payments. That way you'll never have to worry about money again."

"Either way will be fine with me," chimes in another guy, "as long as you don't tell my wife I won."

It turned out that none of them had to worry about how to spend the money. The winning ticket was sold a thousand miles away to a man who had bought his first and only lottery ticket on a dare from a friend.

Thanks to

Josh Oswald and the crew at United Media

The Franklin Stage Company for letting me
    work this out on their stage

The Franklin Free Library for letting me abuse
    my privileges

Travis Williams for the title

All my friends in Delaware County, New York

David J. Krajicek, who pushed me to do this

and

Sue Mullen, who insists I get out of my
    pajamas by noon

8897463R0

Made in the USA
Charleston, SC
24 July 2011